I dedicate this book to Annie my loving wife and devoted partner for
51 years - 1953 – 2004

Without whom this book would not have been possible.

ACKNOWLEDGEMENTS

This book would not have been possible without the work of my late wife (Annie) and my daughter (Elizabeth), who spent many hours researching and typing.

Acknowledgements also go to Charlie Emett, Mrs Jennifer Hamilton, John Moses, Mike Stubbs and their staff at Ink Truck, Printers and Publishers, Carlisle.

James P. Templeton.

Published by Ink Truck

FOREWORD

This book has been a long time in the making and only touches the surface in many places of my father's life.

A conversation sparks another memory and another story to tell. It is amazing what a wonderful memory he has, as I am half his age and cannot remember things that happened last week!

I have no doubt there are many more tales which remain unwritten, who knows perhaps another book will follow in ten years time. I would like to think so.

The printing of this book was delayed due to dad suffering a mild stroke in May 2006 just before it was due to go to the printers, but with his usual determination and the help of many friends, (too numerous to mention – but thank you to you all), he has made steady progress to recovery.

The added hindrance of waiting for cataract operations, which had to be delayed because of the stroke, has added to the delay, but we will still plough on and if indeed you are reading this we have succeeded.

I have learned a lot about my dad's life from helping him prepare this book and have enjoyed the stories related here – I hope you do too.

Elizabeth

INTRODUCTION

James Templeton is a memorable man with a wonderful tale to tell. His words leap from the page as he transports you back to a less frenetic world, where people who were usually financially poorer than they are today were much richer in every other respect. James brings to life folk who were fiercely independent characters who did their own thing in their own way and were not hidebound by political correctness. He leads you through an era in which people were proud to display their individual characteristics, family life was the strength of the nation and the world was a better place because of it. It is a fascinating journey and James is a guide second to none.

At one point in his story he says that he doesn't expect to get a degree, not that that should worry him. For James already has something much more worthwhile: the love, friendship and respect of the people he loves and has served so well: the citizens of Carlisle. That, to James, is worth all the degrees in the world.

For more than 50 years James has had the love and support of his lovely, late wife, Anne, without whom he would not have lived such a fulfilling life. Together they shared their lives through the stirring times related here. These years are laced with lots of laughter, for James has always been able to see the funny side of things, and it shows.

By Charlie Emett

A CARLISLE LAD

EARLY YEARS

I, James Parker Templeton, was born on 13th February 1920, at No. 6 Belmont Terrace in the village of Belle Vue, Carlisle, Cumberland. I was christened on the 24th March 1920 by the Reverend Bramwell Evans (Romany of the BBC) at Caldewgate Methodist Church, Carlisle.

My father, Dan, was a native of Ayrshire, born in Catrine in the year 1880. As a young man he went to the Glasgow School of Art where he qualified as an artist and later became a FRSWS (Fellow of the Royal Scottish Water Colour Society). During his life he painted many pictures in his native Ayrshire and later Cumberland. My mother, Mary Frances Parker, was born in Caldcoates, Carlisle in the year 1886.

Home, 6 Belmont Terrace Main Road Belle Vue Village. (Later 38 Moorhouse Road) Carlisle. (Born in this house 13/02/1920) In the room above the bay window.

Mother and James 3 months old, outside 6 Belmont Terrace 1920.

My childhood was a happy time of my life, well looked after by devoted parents, who would be anxious to see me do well as they had lost a boy (Thomas) and girl (Mary) in infancy, though they seldom spoke of them.

When I was four years old my sister Marion was born on 17th July 1924, this was grand but my first remarks to my mother of 'please can we swap her for a brother' did not go down well!

Life at home was now more active then ever. Everyone from the coalman to the minister and especially the neighbours coming and going to see the new baby. It was a close knit community and everyone helped one another whenever and however they could.

James Parker Templeton age 1
13th February 1921.
Photo by F. W. Tassel

My life continued to be a happy one and I still played in the fields opposite the house and in the open garden at the back where father kept hens and banties along with mother's Border Terriers and Otter Hound and where occasionally 'Darkey' the cat roamed in search of mice.

It seems strange now but my mother kept a pet otter which had been brought up on a bottle when its mother had been killed by accident.

It was a strange pet and would amuse visitors by tunnelling under the carpets in the living room! As it grew older it became rough and too much to handle as a pet so we attempted to release it back into the wild down at the River Eden near Grinsdale but our first attempt was unsuccessful when it followed us home again.

My uncle John and I tried again. We put the otter in a bag and carried it to Grinsdale once again to a spot where other otters had been sighted, this time we were successful. Presumably it found a mate and settled back into the wild habitat where it belonged.

When it snowed in Belle Vue it was a truly fun time. We would gather together as children and sledge down the big hill. The only problem was it was a long walk back up towing

Father, James, the Dog and Cat
1922.

your sledge behind you. It seemed to snow much more when I was a youngster than it does now. Perhaps that is to do with global warming!! I do not think it would be advisable nowadays either even if it did snow a lot, there's far too much traffic on the road.

Let me now describe my native village of Belle Vue. The road then was a rough country road, with a stream down each side,

James out for a walk with Dad
1922.

James, Ayrshire, Scotland 1923.

and a rough cinder path on the right hand of the road going west. From the junction of Burgh Road, where the stream crossed the road, big ash trees grew on both sides of the highway. Coming up the hill to Belle Vue one would pass St Mary's Home and Laundry. This was a Home run by the Nuns for penitent girls and as a small boy I usually ran past this area, because I wasn't very sure about 'nuns'.

James, catching butterflies 1923.

Heading up the hill under the big trees that hung over the path I soon found myself outside the first house (Coalfell - 1894) where the Browns lived. Next came the Jackson's (Bob), then the Jardine's, the Haig's, the Police House and John Byers home. The Templeton's house (my home) came next, followed by the Nicholson's, J Trotter's, the Engine Driver, Cherry's and Errington's, the last house on the row. The next houses on this side were near the top of the hill and Auntie Maggie Stewart's or Old Sandy's and the Post Office which opened in 1890 and closed in 2003.

A view from Belle Vue village looking towards Newtown and Carlisle. Circa 1920.

Photograph taken from No 6 Belmont Terrace 1937.

On the opposite side of the road, next to the orchard, going uphill lived Old Lockhart with his straw hat; then Mrs Carrick, with her old bonnet. Next to her was Belle Vue Mission Hall, where the minister was Reverend Irving; next came Borrowdale's and Farish's and across the gap was old granny Davidson, who was judged by me a 'witch' as she smoked clay pipes and drank gin. Also on that row of cottages we had Wild's; Slee's; Smith's and 'Black Dick Veevers'. If you asked Dick how he was feeling, his reply was, 'I'm dead but I won't stiffen'. Next was the opening to Beaver Road with the old cottages that were once a Pickle Factory. At the bottom end of Beaver was John Allison's house.

Belle Vue 1951. I was born in the house with the canopy, No 6, halfway down the hill on the left.

On Belle Vue hill old Isaac Tweddle lived with his two sisters. He always pleaded poverty, and was never known to spend one 1/2d unnecessarily. He made his own candles for the home, but usually went to bed when it was dark, and got up at the crack of dawn. Many years later he died, leaving a large sum of money, so much for being a 'poor man'.

Living in the next house standing back from the road was Jocky Lister, a railway man. At the corner of Crown Road lived 6ft 4ins tall Jack Elliott and his sister, Maggie. Jack Elliott had a pony and cart which he used for collecting swill for his pigs. The Elliott's were a genuine pair of Belle Vue people. Outside their cottage door stood a big chestnut tree, that spread its branches over the corner of Crown Road and the main road. It was a favourite place for the boys and girls of the village who used to congregate there.

Museum Inn, Belle Vue Village. Circa 1908

Anyone going down Crown Road passed Tommy French on the right and Philip Hare, a gentleman artist, on the left. Further on lived Jimmy Carney, Miss Hetherington, W Rowes, Willie Moffat, McBride's, market gardeners and Thompson's (they ran a threshing machine). Back on the main road stood the local hostelry, The Museum Inn, a quaint old pub, filled with cases of stuffed birds. Spirit were 3d & 6d, for singles and doubles and beer was 2d a pint.

8

Roan's farm House, Belle Vue.

Willie Roans Farm stood at the corner of Beck Road Lonning, where the Dixon's lived and in a cottage opposite them, Mr and Mrs Stalker. The last house in the village was Acredale. Sited just beyond Criffel Lonning where Dick Marshal, Bob and their sister Jinny lived. One day Dick, Bob and Jinny Marshal were in the kitchen, talking, when Jinny remarked that the range was becoming smoky. "The chimney wants a good sweep", she said. Soon afterwards she left the house on an errand and Dick told Bob that this was the time to clean the chimney. So saying Dick got a double barrel shotgun, loaded it and fired both barrels up the chimney. It did the trick. The chimney was as clean as a whistle, but the released soot fell into the kitchen, making every piece of it black, when Jinny returned and saw all the soot the black air turned blue.

In the 1930's there were regular visitors to the Marshal household, they were barn owls and they nested in the chimney stack.

The Marshal brothers were good at Cumberland and Westmorland Wrestling and Dick taught me the art of Clay Pigeon shooting. A cartridge then cost about 1/4 farthing. These were great fellows, travelling miles to wrestle and shoot at village shows etc.

Not far away were some well known farms - Bowmans of Henmoss, Mallinsons of Beaver also Cornhill and Cobble Hall. As a boy I visited these places regularly and of course everyone for miles around knew me. I also helped Willie Mallinson on his milk round, it was great setting off from Beaver with the horse and milk cart. The women used to come to the cart with a jug or basin for a pint or quart of fresh milk 1d, 2d or 3d.

Mr & Mrs W. Jardine nee Maggie Stewart, Belle Vue General Store and Post Office, also a Bakery. 1930. As children we all called her Auntie Maggie Stewart.

Belle Vue 1930. Mr & Mrs Elliott and son Jack lived on the small holding at the corner of Crown Road and Belle Vue road. Jack kept pigs and the pony and cart for collecting swill to feed the pigs.

One morning I remember we were late with the milk, the horse took fright and wasn't too keen after seeing the Graff-Zepplin overhead. With the cash I collected on the milk and other errands I bought a new Raleigh bike for £5 at TP Bells in Abbey Street. This got me into the country much quicker. My next buy was a camera - a 5s Brownie. I soon got the trick of taking good pictures from my father, his tuition stood me in good stead for years to come. He also taught me to swim, because I often went to the river, especially when he was fishing. My mother often used to say to me "Father spends more nights at the river, than he spends in bed". We always had a good supply of trout, herling and sea trout, some weighing as much as 6lbs, 7lbs and 8lbs.

On Saturday nights we could always rely on father being home, just after midnight, because he never fished on the Sabbath. Coming from a long line of Hunting folk, my mother always had dogs, Otter Hounds and Border Terriers. My grandfather the late Tom Parker was huntsman of the C.O.H. and later my uncle John followed in his footsteps and my uncle Joe was huntsman

Mr W. Mallinson and James Templeton delivering the morning Milk to Mother, Mrs Templeton. Circa 1932. The Milk came from Beaver Farm, now Sandsfield Park.

of the D.O.H. So as a very small boy I was brought up amongst dogs, and before the age of 10 years got to know much about otters and the working of hounds in kennels. Our kennels were down the Canal Road off Port Road and I spent many happy days working in my own way, amongst the Otter Hounds, and Terriers. Hunting days for me was absolute freedom. Glorious days never to be forgotten and many a long mile I walked, but never felt weary.

One day I remember well, when news arrived at the kennels that the hounds were invited to Lowther Castle for a week. This was my first meeting with Lord Lonsdale. We chatted about hounds and hunting, at this time I would be 14 years old. ('Lordy' gave me a 2s bit coin which I still have to this day).

Getting back to Belle Vue everyone in the village knew everybody else and they all helped one another in the hard times. I was lucky my father had a good job, being a designer in a Textile Mill, so on a Friday night I usually got a 1d to spend or save. This usually ended up in Auntie Maggie Stewart's shop. Auntie had a good heart for all the bairns, so we always got our moneys worth, even the ones with no penny!

The day came when I had to go to Newtown School. I went at the age of 5 years. This did not appeal very much; it seemed a waste of time. The best lesson was playtime, and time for going home. I suppose I wasn't a bad boy, but had many tricks that annoyed the teachers,

James P. Templeton 1933. Ready for a days hunting which usually started at 7am.

so I often got a whack with the cane, or was sent to Miss Hindson, the head-mistress. On my way home, I often went by the Shady Lonning and over the stiles then down the field, passed the pond, and over the gate opposite my own home. My journey took me past an old hollow tree where I would leave my school books so as not to do my homework – no books – no work!

Newtown Boys and girls school, Newtown, Carlisle. 1928. (James 4th from the left back row).

As I moved on in the school, I was still much the same and 'full of mischief'. I often put bees or wasps in the teacher's desk, or took a cat or dog into school, a mouse or a frog or lizards. These lizards I obtained from Rattlingate Wood and kept them in cardboard boxes. Another thing I was in the habit of doing was catching bats, as they flew low under the trees on a summer evening. They were easy to catch in the Old Mill rafters at Monkhill.

11

Soon the day came when I had to move on to Ashley Street Boys school. By this time I was becoming known as a good school footballer, as I was now a pupil at Ashley Boys and of course got my chance on the sports field. Soon the team showed we could win football games if nothing else, and finally in 1933-34 Ashley had the School Boy Cup. I was still at Ashley Street School when the Master, Billy Shepherd, was pleased for once and remarked 'if you were as good at sums as you are on the sports field it would be great'.

I was reaching the time when I had to think seriously of getting a job and that day finally arrived by chance. I was sent by my mother to Solric Factory (where Dixon's chimney is) to take my father some tea, as he was working late. On the mill stairs I met a well dressed man wearing a pinstriped suit and a bowler. He said "hello young man." My reply was "sir do you know whether there might be any jobs going in this place"? His next question was "Are you Dan's son? Come and see me in my office on Monday morning". Father got to know about this the day after and I don't know whether he was pleased or not. A week later I started work as a textile designer but had to start at the bottom as an office boy with a salary of 8s per week, starting at 9.00 a.m. and finishing at 5.00 p.m. I was now 14 years of age.

James P. Templeton 1934. With Champion Border Terriers at Crufts. The terriers are mother and daughter.

James 1936. Played Tennis for Wigton Road Methodist Church, courts were near the Horse & Farrier, Wigton Road.

J. P. Templeton 1936. Outside right for Albion Rovers Carlisle Thursday league.

I was based on the seventh floor which housed the weaving shed where the Jac Looms were. Cards were used to control the warp threads and pattern on the cloth also the weft thread from the four shuttles of various colours.

Solric made some of the finest materials in the world. These included tapestries which were used to cover seats in Holyrood Palace and chairs on board the Queen Mary.

Between 1934 and 1939 I served my time in textiles at various places:

3 months at Ferguson Brothers

3 months at Morton Sundour

3 months at Cummersdale Print Works

3 months at Albion Mills, London Road

3 months at Waddell's, Warwick Bridge

4 nights at Carlisle Technical College and Tullie House

The Head was a Mr Gardner and Textile Engineer was Sandy Pollock.

I finally qualified as a Textile Designer and Engineer. ATI (Associate of the Textile Institute).

The Office Boy.

A weaver at a Hatersley Loom.

During my training as a textile man I found the job interesting, especially going from one department to another. In the weaving shed a young lad could have a very tough time working among approximately 100 women weavers, but I managed to get along very well and was soon given a new name 'young Dan'.

Next I had to attend the Technical School textile class three and four nights a week. Finally I managed to pass the textile exams in City and Guilds and became an Associate of the Textile Institute (ATI) and Textile Designer.

While at Solric Fabrics Limited my father was also my boss. I still had to 'toe the line' when it came to work and was treated as all the other workers.

13

One day while I was Office Boy a lady came into the main office carrying a large parcel and asked to see the manager.

I knocked on his door saying a lady wished to speak to him; he came to the counter and asked what did she want?

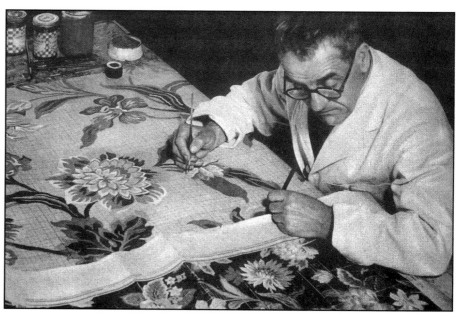

"Father" Dan Templeton. The Boss at work.

The lady opened her parcel of curtains and in a loud voice exclaimed that the curtains had faded and she wished to have a replacement! Just then my father entered the office, his remark was "no wonder they have faded madam they are 15 years old!" He had recognised the pattern as one they manufactured 15 years ago.

The company logo was DEFIUSUN (Defy the Sun). The manager gave her some new cloth for curtains and the lady left, another satisfied customer and the company reputation intact. 'The customer is always right'.

The solric D'Fysun Factory.

While at Solric Fabrics Limited (better known as Shaddon Mills) beside Dixon's chimney, I used to watch the steeple jacks going up and down the ladders and on the top of scaffolding on the chimney itself. On one occasion the man at the top was standing on the edge shouting down that he had left his matches and asked for them to be sent up in a bucket which was attached to a rope. Not everyone could do this job; you certainly had to have a head for heights.

14

The chimney stood at just over 300ft now a little shorter having had the collar and top removed for safety reasons about 1984.

One of the best things about working at the mill was that I was back in football, playing for the firm in the Thursday League with 50 or more other teams competing for the Thursday League Cup and the Hospital Cup. Albion Rovers did well in this league. Our colours were smart black shorts and

Albion Rovers Football Team 1936-37

amber jerseys with black sleeves. This team was in full swing from 1935-1939.

They also serve who only stand and wait.

In September 1937 I joined the St Johns Ambulance Brigade at a cost of 2d per week and before 1939 I held a First Aid Certificate, a St John Medallion and a Nursing Certificate, also a Hygiene Certificate. I did not know at the time but I was to serve St John and the public of Carlisle for 36 years. (This is expanded on in a later section). From 1937 until the war came I took many photographs.

Another vice I had was shooting game. I was lucky to be able to shoot across a very wide area stretching from the Wigton Penrith road at Sour Nook, Hewer Hill, Low House and all along Denton Bottom. Here the river Caldew runs over a rocky bottom.

WAR YEARS

In June 1939, after Solric Fabrics Textile Mill went into liquidation, I took a job with the Carlisle Journal developing and printing department, printing and processing photographs. My pal Alan Norman, who had also worked with me in the Mill started at the same time, doing the same job. We worked at the Carlisle Journal on English Street for many months and had a happy time, until the rumours of war began to be the talk everywhere. Then finally, after a night shift on the morning of September 3rd, Alan and I looked out of the windows across English Street to the Cumberland News Office and read on the placard 'If no word from Germany arrives by 11 am Britain will be at war'. Sure enough war did come. Alan joined the Royal Air Force and was a rear gunner and wireless operator who later won the distinguished Flying Cross and survived after many flying raids over Germany. I was called on to man a First Aid Post my earliest being in Trinity School opposite the Jovial Sailor in Caldewgate. I was now instructing a large cross section of the public in First Aid and manning a new post at Carlisle Swimming Baths, in James Street. This was fine because I could get a free swim any hour of the night and because of the black out we could only use a storm light and candles to light the place.

J P Templeton aged 17 as a young St. Johns Ambulance man in 1937.

Faithful In Difficulties.

By May 1940 my call up papers arrived I had to report to the Lothian and Border Horse. However, when interviewed by the army officer he said 'have you any other qualifications' and of course when I answered 'yes I have a first aid instructors certificate, nursing certificate etc' I was sent to the RAMC (Royal Army Medical Corps) at Eskbank near Edinburgh then to Dalkeith for training, kit etc. After six weeks on the square I became a full corporal in 'C' company as a First Aid Instructor. After a short while I moved to Edinburgh Castle to lecture on First Aid.

My next move was back to Dalkeith as a Corporal Acting Sergeant. We now moved as a full company of men to Glentress Camp, Peebles. We were eventually moulded together with officers and sisters of the QA (Queen Alexandra) as a fully trained unit to become the 59th General Field Hospital. It was now about October 1940 and I was in 'C' company as an NCO instructor and had some real tough lads all from the Glasgow area, Fife and Aberdeenshire, but a few from Birmingham, Liverpool, Ireland and Wales. Once these lads were knocked into shape they proved that they could do the job and we spent many days on manoeuvres in the Border Hills; sometimes out from camp up to six and seven days at a time. The weather began to get very cold and some mornings the frost was so severe our top blanket was frozen to the bed. The Nissan Huts were very cold indeed but a family called Robertson of Eshields took pity on us and often invited some of the lads to their home for a chat, cup of tea and supper. This was a welcome change.

J P Templeton R.A.M.C. outside Glentress Camp near Peebles, Scotland July 1940.

I can now disclose that during my visit to Glentress I was introduced to two sons of Mrs Robertson, Dod and Jock from Eshields who taught me the art of poaching salmon. The Tweed flowed near to Glentress camp and the Robertson's home. During my time off from camp I would go to the river to spot any salmon on the gravel beds this was in the late afternoon. Some days there were a couple of dozen fish ranging from 10

James after a slight Road Accident. I was hit by an ambulance door in the blackout! The driver did not know his door was open. So I was the 1st military patient in Peel Hospital near Innerliethen. I sure got plenty of attention! June 1941

to maybe 30lb weight and on one occasion I spotted a big fish, a really big fish. So I went back to the Robertson men with my report. As soon as it was dark Jock and I set off for the river armed with a carbide lamp and a steel gaff and in the dark we waded in and began to search for the big fish, there was no sign of it when suddenly in the darkness a voice from the other side of the river said "You needn't look for your big fish because you're ower late. I've got the big fish and seven others". The big fish was forty six and a half pound and the small fish among the other seven were about eighteen pound. Not bad for a few hours work before midnight. Of course if you were caught by the bailiff you were in for it - a heavy fine or put in 'clink'. The laugh is that at a later date I was introduced to another of the Robertson men. I said to Jock and Dod "and what does he do for a living" - they smiled and said 'you can guess'. Yes, he was the water bailiff!

Our next exciting moment came when we heard that we might be on the move from Scotland and sure enough I got my first seven days leave. This was the last I would see of my home, and my folks for the next five years. I returned to camp at Glentress to find we were being issued with new tropical kit. And on December 6th we marched to Peebles railway station and joined a troop train. The train moved at a slow speed and stopped at Carlisle Station. Here I saw a guard who lived in Belle Vue so I attracted his attention and flipped a note on to the platform. It simply read 'gone abroad'. But before the guard could get the message a red cap picked up the note, but was good enough to tell the guard the message, so my parents knew I was on my way.

The next stop was Liverpool. Here we left the train and marched to the Docks to board the liner Andes. Andes was the Royal Mail line and a brand new ship. This liner had been commandeered for trooping like all the other big passenger ships. Once on the ship we were allocated

ANDES Royal Mail Lines a new ship in 1940. Carrying troops to South Africa December 1941. This was a lucky ship it survived the War, was refitted and used for cruises.

our quarters on board and we being the only medical unit were asked by the Jaunty who was the Master at Arms to do first aid to the gun crews on the ships. Six inch guns, anti aircraft guns, pom poms and beaufors. I was on the top deck on the pom poms. We sailed from Liverpool as soon as was possible because of the night air raids on Liverpool. Once away from the dock and into the open sea we assembled with the convoy in the Irish Sea. We were now part of a convoy of 37 ships including our protection vessels. Destroyers, Corvettes and the Battleship 'Resolution'. Once round the north of Ireland and into the Atlantic sailing south where we hoped to dodge any lurking submarines then off the Azores we were attacked from the air and bombed. Again luck was with us and only one ship was hit during the attack and five aircraft were shot down. During the next attack we had two more ships damaged and by the following day we were out of range of any air attack, but submarines were still a great danger.

Two days away from the Azores the protection vessels located a submarine and began to throw depth charges. I am not sure whether the submarine was damaged or not. We sailed on towards our unknown destination and at this time many of our lads were down with sea sickness. I was lucky it did not affect me at all even when the ship was ploughing through heavy seas and rolling quite a lot. We soon crossed the Equator and our first port of call was Freetown, West Africa. On our arrival we were met by the natives who sailed out to meet us in their 'bum boats' loaded with bananas for sale. If you threw the money from the weather deck of the ship these lads would dive for the coins and seldom missed any, though there must be many 6d and 1d in Freetown Harbour!

We had been at sea for seventeen days. It was now 21st December, 1941, Christmas was approaching, and we were about to spend the Festive Season in Freetown, not much chance of any snow there, in West Africa, the white man's grave.

The heat was sweltering and humid. Here we took on fruit, fresh water and bananas from the bum boats. No-one was allowed off the ship of course and we left Freetown on 25th December 1941 now sailing free with no convoy. Travelling independently, the Andes moved much faster than in convoy, covering approximately, 320 sea miles a day. Almost before we knew it, Table Mountain could be seen on the horizon.

Photographed at the Sweet Water Canal, Suez.
This was beside the Suez Ship Canal.
Cpl. J Templeton on the walk between the Canals.

We arrived in Capetown Bay where we docked on 1ˢᵗ January, 1942. Still no leave from the ship and we were confined now for several days on board ship until they found out what to do with us. After we left Cape Town we arrived at the docks in Durban 247 miles away on 8ᵗʰ January 1942. To give an idea of mileage Liverpool to Freetown 3701 Freetown to Capetown 3638 miles and Capetown to Durban 685 miles a total journey at sea from Liverpool to Durban was 7754 miles. This was a lucky convoy and only 3 ships were damaged and one lost. Andes was a new liner and a beautiful ship and survived her long trips during the war.

Note of the voyage mileage of the Andes R.M.L.

Left Liverpool December the 8ᵗʰ 1941.

Day 1	8-9ᵗʰ December	travelled		220 miles at sea
	9-10	"	"	292 "
	10-11	"	"	280 "
	11-12	"	"	196 "
	12-13	"	"	286 "
	13-14	"	"	314 "
	14-15	"	"	313 "
	15-16	"	"	323 "
	16-17	"	"	319 "
	17-18	"	"	334 "
	18-19	"	"	335 "
	19-20	"	"	288 "
	20-21	"	"	201 "

December 21ˢᵗ Midday arrived in the harbour at Freetown, White Mans Grave, West Africa. Heat sweltering and humid. Took on fruit including bananas from the 'Bum Boats'.

No one allowed off the ship.

We left Freetown on December 25ᵗʰ 1941 now free sailing, no convoy.

25-26 December travelled			297 miles at sea	
26-27	"	"	326	"
27-28	"	"	321	"
28-29	"	"	322	"
29-30	"	"	319	"
30-31	"	"	305	"
31-1st January 1942			330	"
1-2	"	"	321	"
2-3	"	"	371	"
3-4	"	"	456	"

(What a sight we could now see Table Mountain and Capetown on arrival in the bay. Still no leave from the ship. Sailed next morning 5th January 1942.

5-6 January travelled			142 miles at sea	
6-7	"	"	314	"
7-8	"	"	247	"

Arrived at the Docks in Durban on this 8th day of January 1942.

Liverpool to Freetown	3,701 miles
Freetown to Capetown	3,638 miles
Capetown to Durban	685 miles

Total journey at sea from Liverpool to Durban 7,754 miles.

My report now is in bits and pieces and are recalled to the best of my memory!

Capetown was a real sight all lit up with Table Mountain in the background and the delight for me was seeing the dock cranes with the bold lettering 'Cowans of Carlisle'. After taking on fresh supplies once again we set sail now going south. Andes was now safe from attack and going well in good weather, blue sea and clear sky. From the gun deck we could see dolphins racing along with the ship and flying fish and albatrosses. These frequent the southern ocean.

We were now approaching Durban and on entering the docks again Cowans cranes and several other liners were berthed including Mauretania.

The MAURETANIA
33,200 tons, 68,00 horse power. Length 790 ft. Breadth 88 ft. Depth 60 ft. 6 in.
At the time the Largest Vessel Afloat.

Now what! Orders were again given to change the markings on our luggage we were apparently bound for Singapore, but Singapore had fallen to the Japanese. We were now to leave Andes and assemble on the docks in full marching order including kit bag. (The whole lot in a temperature of 90 degrees in the shade).

Now followed a most exhausting six mile march in the African heat of 90 degrees to reach a holding camp on Clairwood Race Course. Our accommodation was tents and we had ants and other night visitors. During our stay here we did drills, lectures, P.T. etc. and were allowed an occasional pass to have a spree in Durban, visiting the shops and bars. The English shop keepers and restaurant owners usually gave us a free coffee. Our transport from the town to the beach was usually with the Rickshaw man; who was dressed in all his finery. The Rickshaw was a two wheeled covered cart pulled by this fine South African fellow. You got in, sat down and he then set off at a good pace, and you were at your destination in no time at all. Of course you paid before you set off.

Durban beach was a luxury and the swimming was good inside the safe zone where the shark boom was.

While staying at Clairwood camp, a notice went up on the notice board asking for volunteers from the RAMC to do a special 'job'.

One's mind boggles, what job? So with two others I volunteered. I thought this might be exciting or just a fatal mistake. We soon found out after reporting to the dock yard office the job was to treat an outbreak of 'boils' amongst the crew aboard the Mooltan

- a tramp steamer flying the Red Ensign and the following night we set sail, hoping we were going somewhere nice. In due course we reached Trincamlee, Ceylon. No one was allowed off the ship, the cargo was unloaded very quickly and again we sailed on the tide after a very uneventful trip apart from the 'boils'!

We arrived back in Durban Docks and packed up our belongings and medical equipment. The Master at Arms (called the jaunty) came to us and handed over a sum of money as our pay and danger fee! I was speechless to see £35.00 in notes for each of us! The next question – "why danger money?" The reply was that Mooltan was carrying shells and TNT etc. for the war in Burma. 'Oh dear - don't volunteer again'.

We were asked if we wanted another trip to make sure the crew were cured, and a definite answer was given NO. At a later date we discovered the ship should not have sailed at all.

We remained in Durban for another five days. Then a signal came for the 59th to move back to the docks and board Mauretania. This was as you probably know a large liner with four funnels. It was not a very clean ship. This was the first time I had ever seen 'bugs' there were even rats on board, so most of our time was spent in the open, on the weather deck. Slowly, slowly we left Durban and sailed towards the Red Sea and Aden. Here off the coast of Aden with the ship stopped at anchor. The heat at midday was an unbelievable 110 degrees plus. After several days of this, we moved on slowly to Suez and finally disembarked and moved into a camp at El Bala, on the banks of the Suez Canal. This is surely the only place in the world where it is possible to photograph a Ship, a Train, a Lorry and an Aeroplane in motion, all on one photograph at one time!

We camped here for about a month in tents and encountered some of the best thieves to be found anywhere. The 'wogs' could steal under our very noses, even at night they could cut a hole in the tents and steal. One deterrent was to chop their hands with a bayonet and of course the camp guard at night could shoot any intruder – which did

Cpl. James Templeton 7579931 and Boy Cleaners, Sudan 1942

23

happen. These thieves were even caught in the act of stealing a nisson hut, and were removing the corrugated iron from the roof.

Now where were the army going to send us next? Being RAMC and having medical doctors and specialists, our next move was to the Nile Delta Apia - Aswan to await further orders.

Eventually we boarded the Nile River Boat at Aswan and moved slowly down the Nile to Wadi Haifa: 110 degrees in the shade but cold at night. The trip along the Nile was most interesting and the fact that some of the officers including Colonel Mackay, the Commanding Officer, wanted to see the Temples of Edfu and Ramases and other Ancient Monuments we were also allowed off the river boat for sightseeing tours. When we finally arrived down river we boarded a train heading for the Sudan.

The Sudan was a long way away and we were on the train for three days. It was pulled by a huge Garret Engine with a large water tank at the front and its tender full of coal. We travelled at about 20 mile an hour, with stops to make tea from boiling water from the 'engine' and to stretch our legs. The heat during the day was usually 110 degrees to 120 degrees and one had to wear a topee all the time. It was red hot in carriages in day time, even with the dark blue glass blinds pulled down it was unbearable.

With the 59th Field Hospital in Sudan, on special duties! Heat 110°, 1942

Our destination place was to be Gabeit, north of Suakin in Sudan, and this is where we were to be for the next six or so months. Here in the Sudan our job was to deal with any wounded being evacuated south, troops coming from Eratrae and that area and the Air Force base at Summit and so on. Any troops who were very ill were dropped off where we were at Gabit and the few beds we had were used to treat them so they could be moved on soon afterwards. So life was very much routine in the Sudan - military parades and everything had to be spit and polished and so on. The hospital part of it had to run smoothly and like clockwork. I was now Acting Staff Sergeant, again in charge of C Company. We did marches and things during our stay here and guard duties and 'look outs' from the top of the slag heaps which were created from the Gold Mines in that area.

I was at this time in charge of any mail outgoing and incoming and this was collected and put on the train which came through the Sudan once a week. So I was the only one really allowed into the village which again was interesting because the village was taboo to anyone else and I got to know one of the Chiefs in the village and had an interesting talk to him. He spoke perfect English having been educated in London and so on and this was very enlightening - he always pleaded poverty! Then one day I met the District Commissioner who was 'a white' and I told him of the Chiefs plight of being hard up - the Commissioner burst out laughing and said, "hard up, he gets £1 for every mile of railroad that the train passes over every week - which totals some 1,000 miles and apart from that the area over there fenced off and the South Africa Mining Company would not allow him to open it, as he would flood the market and ruin the profits of the Gold Mines". One day it will be opened and he will profit. He also mentioned his seven wives, who all wore their veils and dripped in gold chains and bangles etc. The Chief was a jolly fellow and very interesting to talk to and at one stage his son was acting as a batman in the RAMC camp.

Abu-Hamed (back) the village chiefs son who was bitten by a Camel, with Adrab (front left) and Mustafa (front right).

One day this 15 year old came to request leave from camp to get married - he had made sufficient money from cleaning boots and kit to afford to marry! Several months after he was badly bitten by a camel, he was in a bad way, his wounds festered and the Chief

James with the knife presented to him by The Chief at Gabeit.

told me the Witch Doctor told him he would not live. So one day on a visit to the village I took penicillin and went to give him this. He improved and was soon better, but I was not very popular with the Witch Doctor! When I left the camp the Chief came to me and gave me a treasured possession of his, which was his curved knife out of his belt. I still own this and have it as a memento and reminder of the long hot days in the Sudan and Suakin area. Suakin is on the Red Sea and was where Kitchener in the First World War had his headquarters. The Headquarters are still there to be seen and of course it is known as the Dead City as the port was cut off because the coral grew up and shipping could not get in - yet another interesting place to visit as it was just as Kitchener had left it in the First World War.

This is more or less my time in the Sudan as a soldier. After leaving the Sudan we moved up country back into the desert area and we were now approaching our time in El Alamein. After leaving the desert we moved into Cairo and again we saw the Pyramids and the Mohammed Ali Mosque and we also visited the Sphinx and the Valley of the Kings where the tomb of Tutankhamen was found. So we not only soldiered we travelled about alot. We moved eventually into a rest camp in Tripoli in North Africa. We were still 51st Highland Division - part of the 8th Army and were here

Invitation to Wedding of Abu Hamed which I attended in June 1943.

for a rest, but during the rest period a lot of our heavy kit was taken from us and we were issued with battle order. This was the small pack on your back, the trenching tool and other necessary items required. We were now in battle order. We were taken to landing craft in North Africa and again we set sail heading

Riding Camels in at Suakin.

for an unknown destination, until one morning we could see Strombole smoking away in the distance, so we knew we were heading for one of the islands off the coast of Italy, or Italy itself. This was the landing in Italy.

J.T.

59th Field Hospital Team in Sudan.

26

Western Desert 8ᵗʰ Army.
Photographed from an Army Truck by J.T.
The sappers blew up the petrol dump so that
the Germans could not use it.

After so many years now my memory plays tricks, but I do remember being in Tripoli for about a week. Supposed to be rested, we slept in slit trenches in the open. The date would be the end of August, 1943. We also noticed after a few days, a lot of shipping activity off shore and I remember at this time, an ammunition ship blew up in the harbour I cannot remember the cause of this but it was disastrous. At this time the troops gathering with us were mainly Scots Guards, 3ʳᵈ Coldstream Guards, Grenadier Guards, RASC (Royal Army Service Corps), Kings Own Yorkshire Light Infantry, The Hampshire Regiment, The Royal Corps of Signals and of course the Medical Corps and many more. The next question we asked ourselves was why such a concentrated gathering of troops. Then after a few days we knew for sure that something big was about to take place, but the question was where?

Now the sea area was full of landing craft of all descriptions and we were guessing where we might be going. About the 3ʳᵈ September 1943 we started boarding the landing craft. This was obviously a full scale invasion of the 46ᵗʰ Infantry Division, 56ᵗʰ Infantry Division and the 45ᵗʰ Infantry Division etc. We sailed in the dark and after some time we were told the landing would be at Salerno, in Italy, and the date would be between the 8ᵗʰ and 14ᵗʰ September for us.

The Germans must have been waiting for the landing. The beaches were full of mines and the gun fire was sheer hell. Many of the lads were feeling unwell after being so sea sick. It was now a matter of getting up the 40 or 50 yards of beach as quickly as possible under heavy fire from the German guns, and remember, the beach was heavily mined and many did not reach the beach head. I remember what a relief to be over the beach and into a vacated German gun pit with most of 'C' Company RAMC and several of the 1ˢᵗ Battalion Scots Guards and 3rd Coldstream Guards. By this time the men had some tanks and lorries ashore. We were now on Red Beach.

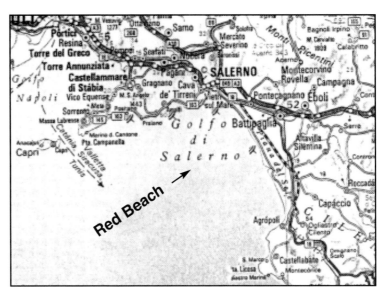

During the late evening we crossed the beach head and went down into the lower ground where tobacco and tomatoes were growing. Beyond that were orchards and some open ground and across the open ground we noticed some buildings, which we thought perhaps to be a farm house but found it was a tobacco factory now held by the Germans armed with mortars and machine guns at every window and a vantage point could be seen all round. I think the following day would be 10th September. What day of the week I can not remember but for the first time we could hear the naval guns from the ships off shore and the shells going over where we were dug in. Then we could see shells exploding on the German positions beyond the tobacco factory on the hill. 15inch shells screamed over later and we learned that these were being fired from HMS Warspite, firing from beyond the horizon some 17000 yards away. I do know now that the ship HMS Nubian fired over 340 rounds from 4.7 guns and her action was typical of the many naval ships off shore. The targets they were shelling were the German tank concentration, German gun positions and positions of the 88mm guns which were creating havoc in the hours of daylight. Also buildings known to be occupied by the Germans. I remember there seemed to be Germans everywhere and from the left of my position the American troops were forced back to the beach and some of the British units were just holding on to the ground we had. The fighting was now violent and the tobacco field I was in with many others was being shelled and mortared and the lads were being wounded and killed at an alarming rate. At this point I, as a medical acting sergeant, had treated many wounded.

The Germans held the far side of the Sele River and blew this bridge. The Engineers put a Baily Bridge across in the dark. But we were still held back by machine gun fire and mortars until finally the Gurka regiment cleared the way.

Along with the staff I had left we managed to get into an orchard and a little bit of shelter amongst some trees in a hollow part of the ground. We could now see German tanks and troops moving in on us. It was late evening and the troops of the 16th Panzer Division came forward pointing guns also an officer with his Luger pistol out of its holster pointing. He informed us in pretty good English that we had to stay put with the wounded and after seeing my Geneva Card, which I still have to this day, he announced 'you are now prisoners of war'.

On the morning of 11th September we could still see the Germans on the edge of the orchard and all that day the pattern of fighting continued and the same confusion and exchanges of territory as gains were made and then had to be relinquished. The Americans were less severely opposed than our lads except further north where 179th Combat Regiment faced the German counter attack in the region of the Sele and Calore Rivers.

Back to our orchard and the 30 or so wounded lads with me, I think the morning of 13th September, as it got light and there were no signs of any German guards near us I said to my pal, "you crawl through the cover of the tobacco to the edge and see if we have any German guards around anywhere." After some time he stood up and waved for me to follow him there, to our amazement, were a Company of the Gurka Rifles brewing their morning cup of tea using solidified meths for heating the water. I shouted, "where are the Germans?" and one Gurka made a gesture with his hand across his throat from left to right. He had a broad smile on his face. This was enough to tell me that they had cleared the Germans from their position. The officer, first sixth, was

British he shouted "you are now free - get the wounded back to the beach and back to the small 59th hospital". This was the 59th general field hospital and the casualty clearing station. Some of us now formed up on field ambulance duties and attached ourselves to fighting units, it was most unusual for a hospital to be so near a battle zone.

Staff Sergeant J P Templeton (7379931) at the town of Orvieto after heavy fighting to take the town in 1943. Note the 8th army flash on the motorcycle and army wagon. (Orvieto is now famous for its wine).

By this time the Hampshire Regiment had suffered many casualties fighting to take the tobacco factory. Also 1st Battalion Scots Guards and 3rd Coldstream Guards and the Gunners. Troops were now in pockets everywhere moving towards Salerno town and our armour was advancing at last but very slowly. We were at this time classed as part of the 56th Infantry Division. Beyond us was the 46th Infantry Division and to our right were the 45th Infantry Division and the 36th Division in the Montesoprano area. In the hills around Altavilla the Germans attacked again and made a stand stopping the Royal Tank Corps from any further advancement.

Moving on, I do not intend to write a war story at this point, but finally in this area I must mention Battipaglia. A fierce street fight took place here. The village was occupied by the 16th Panzer Division and the German Parachute Regiment. They had managed to force the British Troops to pull back out of the town towards Belvedere, but the Grenadier Guards and Coldstream Guards now held their positions just south of Battipaglia and to the left of the Grenadiers were the Scots Guards.

I do remember at this time it was a bright moonlight night as I now lay under the wreck of a wagon with Paddy Glendinning, my Irish pal, and suffering from slight shrapnel wounds. During these first few weeks the Medical Corps had lost many of its men killed and wounded, R.A.M.C. lads from a field ambulance unit.

So now we keep on the move, up Italy along the coast road overlooking the sea towards Capri and Naples.

In the October the 5th Army had suffered and overcome many obstacles. It was reported at this time that the short time we had been here in Italy 20,000 tons of supplies a day were passing through the port of Naples to supply dumps and by the end of October 155,000 tons of supplies and 37,000 vehicles had been landed and meanwhile General Clarks army were continuing their push toward the Volturno River with a total of 100,000 men in advance, Unfortunately, as autumn wore on conditions deteriorated, cold winds and heavy rain made the men miserable and communications became difficult. Some of us only had summer clothing and became very cold especially at night. Vehicles became bogged down in the mud and all the time the Germans kept up a steady artillery attack. The bad news at this time was that the total British and American deaths both naval and army were estimated at 2,350 and a further 7,380 men wounded and 4,000 were listed as missing. Many of these were later to be found in Prisoner of War Camps.

We were now moving towards the town of Fano and on to Forli, still pushing on through the Italian hills towards Orvieto and Cittadi Castello *(see map on page 31)* on to Rimini on the East Coast then up to Forli. Here I was promoted to Acting RSM with 88 MAC. My new posting was to take charge of the evacuated if wounded on route for Naples and Barri.

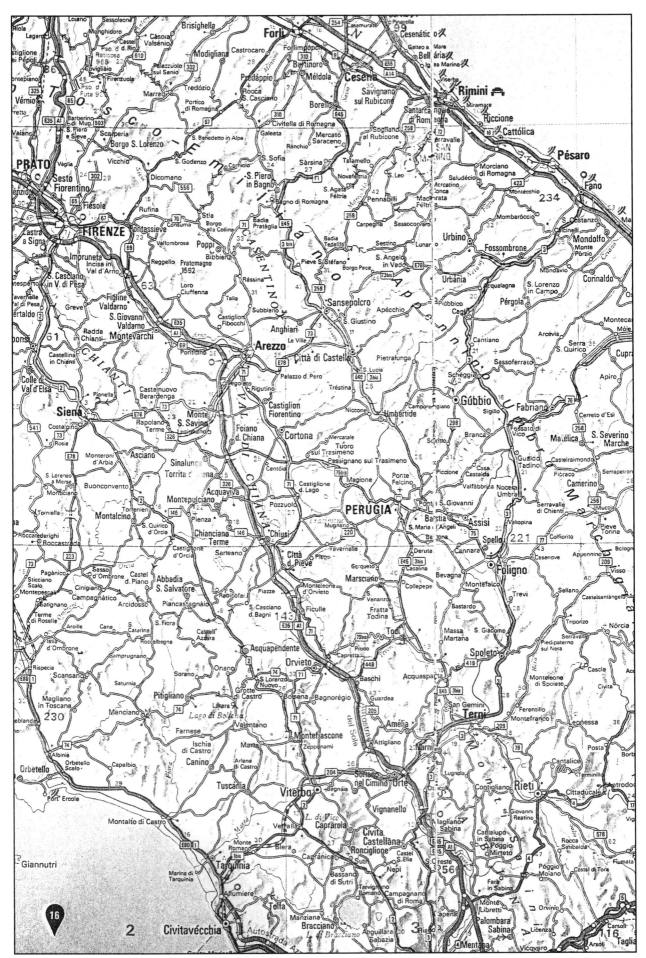

Sgt. J P Templeton in the village of Orvieto, Italy 1944.

While at Forli the Major sent for me to inform me I was due to go home on L.I.A.P. (Leave in Lieu After Python – a code for leave) this was leave after a long period away from home. I said, "OK on one condition. As only one man can go from each unit, and I have just come to the 88th, get a small Italian boy to draw a name from the hat with all the unit names in."

This was agreed and the boy drew the name Templeton. So I packed, ready to leave for home, a unit waggon took me south to Naples to join a ship bound for the UK. Here I met an old pal Bob Wood the cook from the 59th (my old unit) he was also going on leave (L.I.A.P).

So we boarded the liner Duchess of Richmond next stop Malta. Strange things happened from here - the ships anchor was fouled on the bottom of the sea 'stuck' Next the captain of the ship would not sail unless the anchor was free before midnight, because the next day was Friday, 13th - no way would he move his ship on Friday the 13th. However, we did get away before midnight, thank goodness and the next stop we were back in Liverpool Docks.

The troop train was a special train for military personnel only, troops from all the different regiments, and you might say 'war veterans' and some of us still only 25 years old.

Amongst all the troops and baggage was a lone minister and his wife, who finally got permission from the Rail Officer in Charge to travel to Glasgow. He warned them at their own risk be it, and reminded them that they might hear some choice language, as these were men on their way home for the first time in 5 years!

The Duchess of Bedford sister ship of The Duchess of Richmond.
Home on Leave !

32

This couple ended up in the same compartment as Bob Wood and me. The minister suddenly pointed to my kit bag amongst many others on the rack, I said to him. "Is there something wrong?" He said "yes, your name on the kit bag is the same as mine Templeton". I said "Oh where are you from in Scotland?" His reply was "Catrine, Ayrshire". His next question was, "Did they call your father Dan and your grandfather James?" I said, "Yes, and you must be Holy Dan, my father's cousin".

I had been away only a few years but this man and his wife had been away as a missionary in Africa for 40 years.

So we all had a chat and were soon in Carlisle Station; and later they came and stayed with father for a weekend. A strange meeting.

It was very strange coming out of the station. Even the bus stops had been changed. Believe it or not, the conductress was very reluctant to allow me on to her bus because of my army kit. I told her, "Miss I am coming on to your bus whether you like it or not I've been soldiering to keep you on this bus!" She relented.

Next strange coincidence was the surprise when my father boarded the bus at Trinity Church on his way home for lunch: what a joyous meeting after so long.

Mother looked relieved to see me in one piece. Both my parents must have gone through a very anxious time, having lost two children before I came on the scene; and of course my sister Marion was also pleased to see me.

I enjoyed my 14 days leave very much, especially the change in diet. Also wearing casual clothes. But all too soon my leave was up, and I had to don my uniform again and prepare to depart to join my unit again in Italy.

During this leave I noticed a smart young lass had appeared on the scene in Belle Vue. She usually stood at the bus stop near Borderstead at about 8.45 and I noticed she boarded the C14 bus. However time was up. I had to soldier on.

Mother and James.

I hoped she would still be getting on the bus when I got back, as I didn't even know her name!

Once again in Carlisle Railway Station, I joined a special train and several pals on their way down from Scotland. After a non-eventful journey we were back at Gladston Dock, and boarded the Duchess of Richmond ready to sail back to Naples.

The war in Italy during this time was practically over. Eventually I arrived back in Naples, we all disembarked on the dockside and on a large notice board was a display of where all the army units were (approximately).

There was no sign of my unit the 88th MAC RASC Medical Unit, so I enquired at the Military Police on the docks as to the instructions to follow next. The Red Cap Officer remarked, "where did you leave your regiment?" I said "Rimini". His reply was, "well make your own way back to Rimini". I thought he was joking. "You will get lifts, and report to the nearest MP each night" -'typical'!

I did get lifts back up Italy passing battered villages I had seen months before. Finally I got to Rimini but no signs of 88th MAC. A week had now passed. Suddenly, while I was having a glass of vino outside a café, an army supply lorry stopped across the street; one from my lot, 88th MAC. I shouted to the driver "where has the 88th camp moved to?" He replied, "Venice and Udini, get in I am going back with supplies".

On my arrival back I found HQ and reported to the Officer in Charge. He said "Jim don't unpack your kit. We are due to leave for home. "However it was nearly 2 months before our move, so I spent a happy 2 weeks in Venice and the Lido and got to know some of the local people very well. One morning passing along near to the shops in St Marks Square, a smart young Italian lass was busy cleaning a shop window. She said "good morning" (Bon Jurno). I replied, "good morning, what a place, all water and no coffee". So she promptly volunteered to make me a cup of coffee and informed me her name was 'Maria' and her father and family were glass blowers and the shop was full of beautiful

Sgt. J P Templeton 88 M.A.C. RASC. Italy 1944.

glass and china. In a diplomatic way Maria's mother hinted that she could not think of any relationship with a man as she was studying and she was also 1ˢᵗ violinist in the Scala Opera Company in Milan.

I put her mind at rest, and informed her I was on my way home again soon; but Maria made excellent coffee! (I often wonder what became of them).

Sgt. J P Templeton 88 M.A.C. RASC. Venice 1944.
Carrying despatches to the Officers Quarters on the Lido.

A notice was posted on the military notice board asking for men in the area of various units to help at the local remount with horses. These horses had been abandoned when the war was at an end. They required attention, because they had not been properly fed and groomed for weeks. So with the help of some local people and prisoners, I was now in charge of several horses. It was here at Mestri I met Ozzie Coyles, a Whitehaven lad. After the war we sent one another Christmas cards but for 40 years we did not meet. It is only recently we arranged to meet up in Whitehaven – a very memorable meeting.

Sgt. J P Templeton Venice 1944.

These are some of the army Horses rescued during the round up in Italy when the War was almost at an end.

Acting R.S.M J P Templeton. Mestre, Italy 1944.

Here we were again after 3 months packing up to go home. As acting RSM I was told to assemble the lads on parade ready to board a troop train from the nearby railway station, as we were going back down Italy to Bari to fly home. After a very long time on this train and again seeing places we had battered including Cassino we arrived in Bari. A typical military camp with huts and a large airstrip, the planes as I remember were RAF Lancasters. Several days came and went, no flying owing to bad weather conditions and this went on for another three weeks. The planes were grounded so, believe it or not, yes we boarded the train again to go all the way back up Italy to Milan then on to Domadosalo through the Simplon Tunnel into Switzerland and on to Dijon in France. After a slow journey to Calais we crossed the Channel to Dover.

36

I WAS THERE!

We Drove Along the Awesome Road of Death

Through the valley that will be remembered for years to come as scene of one of the hardest victories of the war travelled A. B. Austin, Combined British Press reporter with the 5th Army in Italy. He wrote this grimly vivid story on September 28, 1943 ; shortly after, he and two other famous war reporters lost their lives by enemy action, as told in the next page.

A. B. AUSTIN, world-famous British war reporter, whose last story from the Front appears here. He established a great reputation with his eye-witness account of the Dieppe raid on August 19, 1942. *Photo, Topical*

ALONG the Road of Death we are driving to the Naples plain. The worst is over. We have turned the corner out of the steepest mountains at Camerelle and are heading due east for Vesuvius and Naples. For the past five days of bitter fighting I have seen a mile added to the Road of Death each day. I have driven so many times up and down this valley road through the mountains from Salerno, always just a fraction farther every day, as the infantry struggled ahead, that I can see every piece of ruin and decay on it with my eyes shut.

For years to come this valley will be remembered as the scene of one of the hardest victories of the war. All of us who have written about the fighting have tried to bring home to the outside world just how relentless has been the strain upon the English infantry who have stretched their energy and their courage as far as men can to force a way out of these mountains.

But the result of their fighting and of the German resistance upon the valley itself should be known too, for this is what happens in an invasion and it is not so long since we prepared for an invasion of England. This is what might have happened to any stretch of English countryside leading up from the sea. Along every mile of the lovely valley, from Salerno and Vietri to Cava de Tirreni and Camerelle and beyond, there is not a single house that has not been hit by shellfire or bombing.

WHEN you look from one of its mountain tops you see nothing but peace. The forests drop gracefully down from the high ridges to the vineyards, the orchards and the maize fields. The valley bottom looks as if it were one continuous line of pink and blue and white villas, cottages and farms, swelling every so often into villages and towns. But when you go down among the houses you find that half of them along the roadside are rubble-choked skeletons and the rest are cracked or shell-pocked.

Houses are not the only ruins. Passing along the Road of Death there is first the smashed parapet of the famous Gauntlet Bridge at Vietri. A German tank lies to one side seemingly intact, but shattered inside by the hand grenade dropped from the slope above, which killed all its crew. On the steep mountainside above, a great slash of rust runs through the green trees—the scar on the earth that the German mortar bombs had set on fire.

Every few yards there is some new sign of death and destruction : a German corpse in a ditch, badly needing burial; fallen swollen with death, shattered farm carts ; chimney with a neatly drilled the eye of a rifle; splinters dang-

ling trailing wires across broken walls; graves on high grassy shelves and in ditches—graves wherever a German or an Englishman had fallen, and there was no time to drag him out of the battle, and there are bodies that will, no doubt, be collected before long and buried, in some trim cemetery by the Mediterranean ; the crumbled ruins of futile road blocks—the kind of cement road blocks in which we once placed so much faith at home ; burnt out trucks, shell-craters ; and the rusty litter of German petrol and water cans.

THROUGH it all, up and down every day, stirring the rubble dust into clouds, flattening the shell-cases strewn on the road, bumping in and out of the shell-holes, rumbling across the sappers' bridges spanning arches that the enemy had blown up, moves the traffic of an army, the huge dust-coloured, camouflaged train of trucks and carriers and jeeps and trailers that are needed to supply any force.

Now that the tanks are moving through with all their maintenance train the traffic along the Road of Death has swelled to a roar. Luckily, past Camerelle the single road branches into several parallel roads, so that, at last, we will have elbow room and the Germans have too many different routes to mine or block thoroughly. At the head of it all slowly, methodically, painfully, moves the infantry—laden, dusty men in single file or crawling spread out over the ridges, or digging yet another line of slit trenches to hold a new position.

You come across their small headquarters in ruined houses or under bridge arches ; the Colonel or the second-in-command, unshaven and tired, sitting on the ground with his tin hat pushed back on his head, receiving a stream of messages from the signallers at their wireless sets by his side sending orders forward to his companies

and reports back to brigade headquarters. You find them, if you choose your time tactfully, always willing to explain what is happening with that patience and politeness which is most marked in the front line, probably because men cannot afford to add to the strain by losing control of their tempers.

Threading their way to and fro among all this death, destruction and physical fury are the Italian people. If to this ground struggle were added the terror of air attack this constant movement of people with their bundles and their handcarts might cause great panic and confusion ground. They move away from their homes but however great the ruin they move back as soon as they can. Old, grey men will gravely salute you as they sit in the sun on broken chairs at the doors of roofless houses. Children run among the ruins ; swarms of children pale and ragged, too often with skin diseases. Whenever you stop small boys run up to your jeep, begging cigarettes.

Mothers sit on fallen blocks of stone to suckle their babies. Old ailing women are

LAST STAGE IN THE BATTLE FOR SCAFATI BRIDGE, which A. B. Austin and his colleagues, Stewart Sale and William Munday, saw but did not live to report. Story of how the three met their fate is in page 346. British infantry men are here waiting for a glimpse of the enemy holding positions in houses on the other side of the river and from where machine-guns were trained on the bridge. *Photo, British*

PAGE 345

37

ON THEIR LAST ASSIGNMENT, William Munday (right background, hands on hips) and A. B. Austin (standing behind Munday) watch German prisoners—one wounded by Bren-gun fire and supported by his comrades—being brought into Scafati underguard. Shortly afterwards they and their colleague, Stewart Sale, were killed by a shell from an enemy tank, as told below by Basil Gingell, who was standing beside them but miraculously escaped. *Photo, British Official*

trundled past on handcarts wrapped in their bedclothes till they can be trundled back again in safety. Now and then someone is killed or dies in the normal way. Along the Road of Death, grotesque because it is the last thing you expect to see in a battlefield, comes the undertaker's hearse, with black hangings and plumed horses. The one thing you never find is resentment. Their homes are ruined their lives disrupted, yet they greet you amiably, grin and wave from broken windows, talk as long as you will let them. Either life is easy to rebuild in the Mediterranean warmth or they feel our march along the Road of Death is the last battle of this war.

I Saw a Shell Kill Three War Reporter Friends

The death by enemy action of three front-line war correspondents with the 5th Army—Stewart Sale, William Munday, and A. B Austin (who only a few hours before wrote the story in page 345)—was witnessed, and nearly shared, by Basil Gingell, of the Combined British Press. His account of the tragedy, dated October 1, 1943, is given here.

WHEN the Italian landing was planned and Press representation was apportioned I found that Austin, Munday and myself were attached to one beach-landing party and Sale was with another party. It was therefore not until after we had set foot on Italian soil that I met Sale again, but the other two were my constant companions throughout the fighting that has taken place along that section of the Salerno bridgehead held by the British.

And I was with them when they died. With the narrow foothold such as we had at the beginning along the Gulf of Salerno, it was obvious that we were never out of range of enemy fire, for the front line was on our doorstep. Although always anxious to see battles at close quarters, it is no part of a war correspondent's job to take foolhardy risks, and all three were not only keen reporters but level-headed men.

When the break-through along the Cava Valley gained momentum Austin, Munday and myself, who knew of its imminence, joined in a procession of the armour. We reached Scafati well to the fore, but while the units pushed on over the bridge we waited behind because of snipers and machine-guns that were trained on the bridge.

We had lunch by the roadside, and while sitting there we saw Stewart Sale and Frank Gillard of the B.B.C. drive by. We hailed the new arrivals, and as the traffic moved over the bridge we decided to walk down. We had covered perhaps 200 yards, Gillard and Sale walking on ahead, and Austin, Munday and myself following. Sale stopped to look in an air-raid shelter that was in the main street, and Gillard said he was going on and crossed the road. By this time we had joined up with Sale and we stood at a street corner looking down the road. There was some general banter about the front line.

The four of us were standing in a little group in space no bigger than a hearthrug when I saw a terrific flash ahead. I heard no sound of gunfire, but the next second I felt myself bodily flung up the side of the track for more than fifty yards, while debris and dust rained down on me. I had no idea what was happening, but groping my way out I returned to the corner and there found my three companions lying as they had fallen. An ambulance attendant who darted in asked me to help him, but when he took a second glance he realized that all three were dead. He darted off to attend to others, while I stood back against the wall suffering nothing but a few scratches.

Shelling and machine-gun fire broke out, ranging on the corner where the four of us had stood. Some Italians took me to their home and there I stayed until morning. A sharp battle raged round the area throughout darkness, but in the morning my three friends were buried by the roadside where we had had our lunch on the previous day : where Austin had said that he had a story that would write itself and Munday had made his plans for the following day.

Over their graves are planted three wooden crosses made by our jeep driver, who had taken Austin, Munday and me over many miles since we landed and has himself seen more than the average share of excitement out here. There they remain, with Vesuvius in the background, until such time as all those killed in this bitter fighting in Italy can be gathered into some central resting-place.

From England I Went East to Join Paiforce

Life on a troopship and with Paiforce (which stands for Persia and Iraq Force) is vividly described by a member of the Amalgamated Press—now L/Cpl. Lewis Hulls, of the Royal Corps of Signals. Names of places on the journey are omitted for security reasons.

WE were very crowded on the troopship— a converted liner—but not too uncomfortable. We slept in four-tiered bunks, and fed at tables seating eighteen men. The food was pretty good, the white bread and fresh butter being a particularly welcome feature. Hot sea-water showers were always available for bathing, but attempts to wash clothes in these showers ended in

dismal failure ; for that job we had to use our rationed supply of fresh water.

Queues were an important part of life on board ; we had queues for the canteen (wh such luxuries as tinned fruit and milk c late could be had), for baths, for bar concerts, for fresh water and f After settling down, we started regular routine programme doing P.T. and route m

The ambulance attendent mentioned in this reort was Jim Templeton.

Home again - not quite!

We were now transported to Aldershot Barracks and after a short while three more Warrant Officers and myself were told to report to the War Office for special duty. Our duty was to report to Records Office at Barons Court and check that all the demob papers were properly signed.

This was a cushy number for a while, and if you had relatives in London you could get a 'sleeping out pass' - so I applied for a pass and stayed with Maggie Woodhams a friend of the family. So every day I travelled from Plumstead to Barons Court.

The end of World War II acting RSM J P Templeton in Records, Barons Court, London to supervise the signing of Demob Papers. Circa 1947.

R.A.M.C. Records Office J P Tenpleton and civilion staff.

During my stay in London I applied for a vacancy on the Metropolitan Police Mounted Section and was more or less accepted. However my father sent me a copy of the Cumberland News indicating a vacancy for a full-time Ambulance Man was coming up soon in Carlisle.

I applied but remember I still had to be demobbed from the Army. I was now back in Edinburgh Castle to collect my demob papers. The army never did things the easy way 'oh no'! I was to go down to York to be demobbed and, following, that I went for interview for the Ambulance vacancy in Carlisle and found there were forty applications.

However when I was short listed in the last three, my hope began to look bright, I was called in before the Panel of the Employers Council Health Committee or whatever and one councillor remarked. "You are right for the job. The only thing we find not in your favour is that you are too young". 'Sink or swim' my immediate reply was "I wasn't too young to drive ambulances in the Western Desert".

At this point Dr J Lamberton asked me to leave the room I thought I'd blown my chances. After a few minutes he called me back in and told the others they could leave. He smiled and said you have the job.

Next I had to have my driving test with Norman Jackson from the Police Office. I passed this, so now I was a Carlisle City Ambulance driver with the good wage of £4.19s.0d. per week.

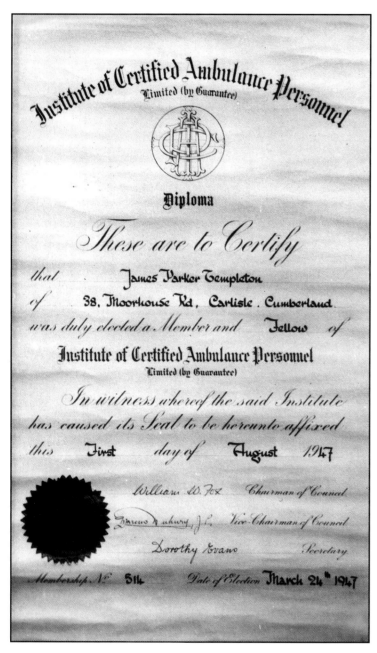

The highest First Aid Certificate posible F.I.C.A.P.
Jim was the first man in Carlisle to gain this
Certificate in 1947

The Ambulance Service consisted of 2 ambulances and 6 men based at Fusehill Hospital. My workmate was Bob Richardson and we worked a 3 shift basis. The set up until about 1949 when the Council decided the ambulance service would be amalgamated with the City Fire Service and operate from the Fire Station at Warwick Street, about 1951. Me being the youngest ambulance man I was given the chance to go to the Fire School and train as a Fireman at Felling, Northumberland, and after 3 hard months at the Fire School I became Fireman J Templeton. So now Robert Todd, the Fire Chief, could use me for fires or ambulances, and of course my pay was more, and instead of retiring at 65 years of age I would retire at 55.

During my working life at Warwick Street Fire Station I enjoyed every minute, my work mates were first class and don't forget we were nearly all ex service men and I would say Carlisle Fire & Ambulance Service was one of the best in the Country. During my 25 years I attended both fires and road accidents. It would be a marathon task to go into the working life of a Fireman; but I did publish a book entitled '100 Years of Carlisle Fire Brigade'.

I would like to point out I must be one of the few firemen that <u>never</u> joined the Fire Service! I was transferred from the Ambulance Service to the Fire Service, the move of course turned out good!

Now on the Fire Station and being a keen photographer I took many photographs of fires and anything relating to the Fire Brigade.

No doubt it will be of interest to quote one or two characters that became well known to the ambulance men and the police. Most of them were harmless - they were the Saturday night lot.

Mrs X, for instance, would nearly every Saturday night be picked up by the City Accident Ambulance - she was full of abuse, but as I said before harmless. One early morning I got a call from the police to the Lowther Arcade. Inspector Sloan was standing with Mrs X in the Arcade and our friend was the worse for drink! When she saw me appear her remark was "Oh Hell, here comes trouble!"

I said to the Inspector that she had a deep cut on her head and asked how it had happened. He laughed. "She says a double decker bus knocked her down in the Arcade".

Fireman J P Templeton - taken during a demonstration.

I bundled her up to casualty - the language was choice, especially when the Doctor stitched her wound. The annoying thing then was the ambulance staff had to see her home. On her arrival at her house her son opened the door. His remark was, "what's happened to her now?" I said, "she reckons a bus ran her down in the Arcade." His reply was choice - he said "I wish she would stand on the railway and get run over by the Royal Scot."

One has to smile now!

Maggie in Willowholme was another character she had usually been drinking gin and meths and after many jaunts in the ambulance or black maria she finally died in her sleep!

If they weren't in bad shape, the policeman would bundle them into the house and warn them not to be seen out again! I for one did a lot of things then that would be unheard of now!

After serving the public for 20 years on Ambulance and Fire I finally retired from the Brigade following a road traffic accident when I strained a heart muscle getting someone out of a wagon. I was regarded to be unfit for active duty so did not attend accidents or fires due to my condition, but saw out my days on nightly switchboard duty. I retired on the 1st July 1973 about the same time the Fire Brigade became Cumbria Fire Service and the Ambulances were back on their own again now, Cumbria Ambulance Service.

I was now recovering to a degree from my heart problem but had to look for a 'light job' according to the doctors! So I worked for a short period in the Store at Metal Box, James Street, but this was not that 'light' and again I was having heart problems and after much hassle and debates I was finally put on invalidity.

I must state here the most degrading experience of my life was walking into the Labour Exchange, the staff were far from pleasant. They looked at you as though you had never worked in your life!

It was at this period I also had to retire from St John Ambulance Brigade, at the rank of County Officer, after serving the public for 35 years.

'ST. JOHN' OFFICER RETIRES
AFTER 35 YEARS

Mr James Templeton, of Newtown Road, Carlisle, a well-known St. John Ambulance Officer, retired this week after 35 years service.

"I had just turned 17 when I decided to join the service. There wasn't much to do in those days — no TV or anything and I wanted to learn some first aid", he said.

While with St. John Ambulance Mr Templeton was chiefly concerned with the instructing side of the work.

"I would have retired five years ago but decided to stay on, but now I am definitely retiring", he said. "I've not yet decided what to do in my retirement but my work on the pictures of old Carlisle for the "Evening News and Star" "Those were the Days . . . ." column on Monday evenings, keeps me pretty busy.

"The collection must be the biggest collection of pictures of old Carlisle in any one place. The number is rapidly approaching the 500 mark. People have sent them in from all over Cumberland. It's a great challenge — there was one picture which had lain in a barn, it was torn in half and had to be joined and made into a new picture. Sometimes it takes as long as a month before a picture is in any shape to let people see it".

Cumbrians — and there must be many of them who know Jim Templeton — will remember his fantastic "scoop" picture in 1964 — when the "spaceman" appeared on a photograph he took of his daughter on Burgh Marsh.

"That picture — which was in colour — is now in the Science Museum in Tokyo and has been included in the Children's Encyclopeadia of the U.S.A."

This year will mark a double retirement for Mr Templeton — August will see him retire from his full-time employment as fireman with Carlisle Fire Service.

MR TEMPLETON

42

Mrs Robertson and I just after the War 1948.

Photographed at the Nook Farm, Southerby, nr. Hesket-New-Market while helping with farm work and young collie dogs. 1950.

43

ANNIE RUTHERFORD

Now I have returned to Carlisle my first priority was to watch and see if the smart young lass was still about at Borderstead, and still travelling on the C14 bus. I soon found out she was and noted she seemed delighted to see me on the same bus again.

After several journeys I went and sat beside her, our journeys to town were too short, so I asked her would she like to go out to the Palace Cinema (the Palace because it had several double seats!).

Our night out was a success. I remember the film was Spring in Park Lane.

After several outings we began to see each other quite often, living in the same area, me in Belle-Vue and Anne in Borderstead. We had many happy days courting and about 1952 we got engaged, and it was at this time we planned to get married.

Annie (Anne) Rutherford was born at Tullie Street at her parent's house on 30th April 1929. She was christened by Canon Wilson at St Cuthbert's Church, Carlisle where we were later to marry.

Later they moved to 8 Holywell Crescent, Botcherby and at the age of 5 she attended Botcherby Infants School and later Brook Street School. She started work at the age of 15 in the Millinery Department in Bullough's Shop on Castle Street earning 10 shillings a week. She was always well turned out in her black dresses and black shoes, which she had to buy herself, the 'uniform' of the job.

Photograph of Anne taken by James 18/06/1950

Annie did well at Bullough's and was promoted twice, often asked to model fur coats, hats, suits and dresses to show potential customers.

Later Annie and her parents moved to Borderstead at the junction of Burgh Road and Moorhouse Road, where she was living when we first met.

44

During our 'courting' days it was a pleasure to spend Sunday afternoon, especially if it was fine, walking our favourite route, which was Burgh Road to Grinsdale Bridge, down into Grinsdale Village to the 'coops' and back along the river bank to Grinsdale Church where we often stopped, sometimes to picnic. Then on through the Village over the style and back to Knockupworth through the farm yard and back onto Burgh Road to Borderstead.

Another route we walked was along Moorhouse Road as far as Rattlingate Lonning through the wood past the scout camp then joined the 'triangle' road and back onto Burgh Road.

We carved our initials on trees at Rattlingate and also on the bridge at Hosket Hill where we often used to sit. These were still visible when I was last past that way!

These were enjoyable days, cars were not a problem and life seemed less hurried.

On the 24th March 1953 we were married at St Cuthbert's Church by Canon Wilson and the Reverend R Brown. This was the first time a wedding ceremony had been performed by a Church of England Minister and a Methodist Minister permission having to be granted by the Bishop.

The Very Reverend R E Brown Methodist and The Very Reverend Canon Wilson Church of England outside St Cuthbert's Church 1955

James and Anne 24th March 1953

The day was glorious warm sunshine, we held our reception in the Co-op Botchergate, and left for our honeymoon in London on the 3.40 p.m. train. We arrived in London and booked in at the Strand Palace Hotel; and spent a happy week seeing the sights. The flags in London were all flying at Half-Mast as Queen Mary had died on 24th March 1953.

45

After our honeymoon we came home and rented No. 3 Port Road, not much of a house, but our home. Renting was a mistake, we should have put a deposit on a new house – but we all make mistakes!

Anne left her job at Bulloughs when we married and devoted her time to home life (which was the done thing then). I was working shifts so this was easier and meant we saw each other more too.

While at Port Road our first two daughters were born, Frances, was born 10th July 1954 and Elizabeth 5th October 1958.

We eventually moved to our own house, 201 Newtown Road at a cost of £2,000.

This was a happy home and our third daughter Anne was born 10th September 1968.

Then a sad event, Anne's mam died, and her dad came to live with us.

After living with us a number of years Anne's dad (Thomas Rutherford) died. He was a pleasant, quiet man, clever at his work as a master joiner and cabinet maker. Sadly in his later life he suffered Parkinson's Disease.

In the year 1994 we made our second move and bought our new bungalow in Coledale Meadows and Anne and I enjoyed nine very happy years together there, working and living in such a pleasant place, and in 2003 we celebrated our Golden Wedding, 50 years together.

Anne had been unwell for some time but took a disastrous turn for the worse and on the last day of August 2004 departed this life aged 75.

So now with the help of my three daughters, I just have to soldier on, and keep working as before, but its hard work sometimes without Anne's drive and backing.

Its certainly true, behind a good man, there usually is a good woman: I think her motto was 'if you can't beat em join em', and a splendid job she did!

Mr and Mrs J P Templeton Circa 1970.
Taken in the garden at Belle Vue.

Taken at our golden wedding Party .
50 years married.

FIRE BRIGADE YEARS

I was chosen to represent the firemen of Cumberland and Westmorland on the Armistice Parade at the Cenotaph in London on 9th November 1968.

I reported to the Royal Hotel, Woburn Place, Russell Square, London WC1. Here I was booked in for one night's stay along with firemen from all the different counties.

Shortly after booking in at the Royal Hotel three London Firemen arrived all carrying 100 foot ropes, this aroused our curiosity and when we asked why they needed the rope at the Hotel they informed us that having attended so many London fires and rescues they were making sure they would have means of escape if the Hotel had a fire during their stay.

We made a note of their room number and its proximity to ours and settled down for the night.

Next morning we reported for duty and inspection on the parade ground for first inspection at 7.30 a.m. by Prime Minister, Harold Wilson, Mr Callaghan, other members of the cabinet and senior fire officers.

After a break of tea and sandwiches we were back on parade for the second time at 9.00 a.m. We marched a short distance to the Cenotaph ready for the 11.00 a.m. parade and wreath laying.

Fireman James ready to leave for London to represent the firemen of the North on the Armistice Parade 9/11/68.

It was a cold morning but I was well prepared having taken a tip from an old fireman who told me to keep my pyjama legs on under my uniform trousers and it certainly did the trick.

Fire Brigade Tales

Red Watch

Days on duty varied very much, never two days the same but the same crew of firemen on the Watch. The officers were a 'good bunch' and could give and take a lot of 'stick', hilarity and pranks.

A sub officer on one night watch began to give a lot of orders – 'you will do this or else', so to shut him up, the lads tied him up on his bed with a 50ft line and carried him out into the station yard: a bitter cold night. On hearing the commotion the Station Officer appeared and shouted 'what the H is going on'. Robo our spokesman replied back 'don't worry we are stocktaking'.

Another night a woman was reported to be in bed in the men's dormitory, and sure enough it seemed like a blonde. A report was conveyed to the officer of the Watch, he would attend to the matter without delay. Indeed a woman on the station premises at 1.00 a.m. It was later

Red Watch, Carlisle 1956.

discovered that a certain constable from next door had found this 'female' outside one of the city dress shops, carried it down Scotch Street into the fire station. The 'woman' in question was a redundant shop mannequin!

This was a chance that could not be missed by a group of lively firemen. Next day the news reached the Chief, Mr Todd and a certain few were given a dressing down (but with a smile).

We had an elderly lady as day cook, who could be a bit bad tempered or crabby. I suppose she had reason to be sometimes, because we could wind her up!

One lunchtime Fosh and I walked into her kitchen and we did the wrong thing, we said 'Mrs F can you warm these pies without burning them'. She promptly knocked the pies off the plate, downed tools (and 'fag') and went to Mr Todd the Chief with her pie story, that these two firemen walked into her kitchen and passing remarks about the ability of her cooking etc.

Not much time after the 'tanoy' went 'fireman T and fireman F report at once to the Chief's Office properly dressed!'

We reported entered and stood before the Chief he looked up in silence, then carried on writing, after 3 or 4 minutes he looked up and laughed! 'Look you two don't upset the cook anymore or she will stop my cups of tea and soup, get back to your work and don't let me see you in here again'.

James Templeton No. 40
City Fire & Ambulance.

Another prank that comes to mind reached a point of no return.

We had a lady who came in on the day Watch to cook dinner, a Mrs A. She decided because the weather was very hot she would make a lemon jelly for the sweet, and in order to get it to set she would put it below the bed in the dormitory, next to the Pole Hatch (where we slid down the Pole) and the cool draught would help it to set quicker.

During the late morning a small group of the firemen (no names, no pack drill) remarked look at that it looks like 'pee'.

A decision was made they would draw the attention of the sub officer to come and see 'this' below the bed.

Hook line and sinker he took the bait! Toilets were a few feet away and some lazy so and so has to use a pot and left it here. Now the station officer appeared, " 'tut-tut' get the men on parade immediately."

At this point we had to back down and accept defeat with a severe telling off and a hard fire drill for about 2 hours.

Many times a very unnecessary soaking either from bucket of water or the hose took place because of some chance remark; all in good fun.

I walked in one morning and was delighted to tell everyone Anne and I had got another daughter, the third one. Don't believe a word he says remarks Big Jim R then Fosh piped up I saw Anne a month ago. I remarked 'no, its true!.' At this point they grabbed me and put me in the cold bath fully clothed and Robo actually went to see the new baby!

Sunday was usually a stand down and of course we hoped there would be no fires so we could have a bit of recreation; darts, snooker, table tennis or rounders in the yard.

This particular afternoon sport ended spectacularly. Walter scored a direct hit during the rounders and the ball went through 'Ma Pats' front window. It's a good thing she was a sporty person. A collection was taken 2/- each and Walter put the new glass in the front window.

In another episode the same three firemen JT, Fosh and Robo attended a farm fire. The out buildings consisted of byres, stables and store rooms on the ground floor and the whole of the loft above was well alight. While water was being hosed onto the fire, we happened to ask the farmer was there any animals still in the building. 'Oh yes, a large bull, but I wouldn't bother trying to get him out he could kill you!'
So we had a peep at the animal and decided to rescue the beast. It was tricky to say the least.

Carlisle Fire Brigade Staff 1950. Photograph by J P Templeton

Robo said 'you take your coat off and put it over his head so that he can't see us'. We could hardly see or breathe for the smoke! So we got Fosh to put his coat over the bulls head and I managed to put the point of my axe through the ring in his nose. Robo pushed the axe but now the problem was could we back him out of the stall (a one ton bull). However he behaved not so bad, but once he reached the door and could smell fresh air we scattered out of his way. No thanks from the farmer except to say we were all daft and he went to bed in the middle of all that was going on and he wouldn't even boil water to make tea!

It's a good thing we are all different, even if some of us are a 'bit daft'.

The Fire Station by this time had several Royal Humane Certificates on its walls for the rescue of animals from floods and fire!

Carlisle Firemen on the Armistice Parade. Circa 1953.

While attending the Leading Fireman's Examinations at County Durham the applicants were interviewed and tested on various subjects. You passed along several Chief Officers sitting at a table and you would be asked questions for five minutes. These officers had their 'pet subjects' and one officer in particular was C V Hall, Chief of Durham County, known to a great many Fire Brigades as being very strict regarding First Aid.

I remember the first chief asked me questions on Appliances, the second one on Hydraulics, now came number three Mr Hall. I sat on the chair ready for his questions.

At this period of my position as a fireman I knew the St John First Aid Book from cover to cover.

Mr Hall looked up at me and remarked 'I am going to see what you know about First Aid' –

Question – "What do you know about First Aid?"

Answer – "I know everything in that First Aid book in front of you."

His monocle fell off – it was now a battle of wits.

"Right", he said "we will see how clever you are"!

He asked me about burns and scalds and as he turned the pages I said to him – "you will find these on page 98".

He picked a different subject – again I told him which page to turn to.

Time was up and the bell went to move on.

At the end of the exams he sent for me and congratulated me on my knowledge of First Aid. His remark was I have never met anyone who could quote the St John First Aid Book word for word.

He gave me a pass mark of 98% - two marks deducted for cheek!

Overall I did not do so badly and returned to Carlisle still as a fireman and Mr R Todd, Carlisle's Chief sent for me to his office. He wanted to know what I had done to Mr Hall. First Aid was his 'pet' subject but he had certainly met his match.

A second trip to London with the Fire Brigade First Aid Team saw us progress through to the final in Reigate, Surry to compete for the gold cup trophy. We managed to get to the final, beating Kendal, Preston, Lancaster Blackpool and Birmingham on the way.

We finished second by one point, being beaten by Bristol.

J P Templeton with the Morris HH 7020 and Bob Richardson with the Austin HH 290.
Taken at the rear of Fusehill Hospital 1948.

FIRE AND AMBULANCE BRIGADE NOTES - UPS AND DOWNS ON DUTY

In the years of service with the fire brigade my colleagues and I were called to many events, some humorous and others extremely sad.

We rescued various animals, cats from trees and drains, cows from mud banks cut off by incoming tides and dogs stuck down holes.

Children were often in trouble too one particular boy I remember wedged between a lamp post and a brick wall. He had climbed up the lamp post and slid down, but the wall was closer at the bottom than the top and his leg had become wedged tight. Gentle coaxing and a bit of grease did the job and no harm done.

J P Templeton (note the City badge).
One of the first Carlisle City
Ambulance Drivers 1948.

Having a camera with me most of the time was often a drawback. In those days there was no official photographer for the police and being housed next to them on Corporation Road I was often called upon to photograph bodies taken from the river or victims of fires or traffic accidents. One tragic victim was cut down by a wagon while he was working in a manhole near to Eden Bridges, it was cordoned off but the wagon driver had not seen it in the dark.

On a lighter note an elderly lady in her eighties left the road at Wragmire Bank corner just outside Carlisle, shot through the hedge with her Bently car, took the bark off a tree, rolled the car over and back onto its wheels. Her injuries were minor cuts and bruises and when I arrived she was sitting by the road having a smoke! I asked her what had happened to which she remarked – 'oh I'm not sure, I was doing about 90 mph and left the road'.

She was not too concerned about herself or the car but the fact that she had lost her dog, a rare Pomeranian, in the accident it had ran away. She offered the policeman a reward of £5 to anyone who could find the dog. It turned up several days later in Low Hesket and was duly returned to its grateful owner.

A letter of thanks arrived at the Ambulance Station a few days later with her thanks.

This tale had a happy ending but others over the years have been very harrowing indeed. We dreaded the call to a car smash and worse still a car on fire after an accident, but the worst possible was when parents in a car are killed and the children are left behind.

I still read road accident reports in the papers and my heart goes out to the victim's families, but we should also think about the trauma the rescuers have to go through as well. They live with the images and pray they never see the like again, but they do. They go home to their families who know, as mine did, when they have had a bad shift.

J P Templeton 1949 with the new Bedford Ambulance. Taken just before the Ambulances were taken over by the City Fire Service.

James, Carlisle City Ambulance, 1950.

City of Carlisle

Ambulance Service

Presented to

Ambulance Driver
J. Templeton.

in recognition of
meritorious service rendered
in the course of duty
on the 19th August
1950

J H Partridge

Mayor.

ST JOHN'S AMBULANCE BRIGADE

When I joined the St John's Ambulance in September 1937 they held their meetings in one of the Old Lanes off Scotch Street – I think it was Globe Lane.

The meeting was in an upstairs room and at that time there would be a class of about 40 men.

The Superintendent at that time was a gentleman called Mr Stamper, and the Doctor giving the lectures was Dr James Lamberton M.O.H. To become a member it cost 2d a week and after the Doctor's lecture you were taught the practical skills of First Aid.

As you progressed through you sat an exam each year, one oral and one practical. After 3 years you were awarded the St John's Medallion and a bar each consecutive year after and this meant you were qualified for public duties.

The Johnathan Gray Challenge Shield.
Won each year by the top Ambulance Man.

James and Marion Templeton.
Brother and Sister completed 60 years
service with St. John Ambulance.

Race meetings, sports events, theatre, cinemas and all manner of public functions. The more public functions the more public duties you did the more experience you gained.

I never dreamt I would serve as a St John man almost 36 years, serving on average at two public functions a week.

Once a year was the Annual Inspection attended by the Higher Officers of St John, London along with doctors from Cumberland and Westmorland.

The most memorable parade and inspection was held on Fitz Park, Keswick which was inspected by Lady L Mountbatten and she chatted to me for at least 10 minutes regarding my Army ribbons and various places I had been.

I was promoted to 2 stripes which I held for 16 years then 3 stripes, then Divisional Officer and finally County Staff Officer and Secretary for Cumberland.

J P Templeton County Staff Officer St. John Ambulance.

Lord Lonsdale and Dr. Moffat asking questions about the Medical Corps work in Italy and the Army R.A.M.C.

> ## This incident, writes the Surgeon-in-Chief, has a real touch of the country about it

★

Rider to Hounds Displays His Skill as First-Aider

CORPORAL J. TEMPLETON, of the Carlisle Ambulance division, is a keen follower of hounds. He was out not so long ago in open country and had fallen behind the hunt when, from across a narrow river, he heard the sound of someone in pain.

He got across the river and found an elderly man lying awkwardly after a fall of about 20 feet. He was dazed and shocked. Later examination showed he had a compound fracture of the left tibia and severe chest bruising.

No first aid material was available, and the nearest main road and house were a mile away, but Corporal Templeton got to work. Handkerchiefs were used for temporary dressings, whip-thongs and neckties served for limb immobilization. Corporal Templeton took off his jacket, borrowed others from the huntsmen and with hunting poles rigged up a serviceable stretcher. The patient was carried carefully over the difficult ground and calmed when he came to on the journey. At the house he was given stimulants, and it was not long before they got him to hospital. There, the house surgeon spoke highly of the emergency treatment.

The Surgeon-in-Chief at Headquarters, hearing of this account of Corporal Templeton's service, praised his " serene and efficient adjustment to circumstances ".

Major White Knox added : " I know of a somewhat similar case where with unskilled handling a girl became a cripple for life. It is most satisfying to Brigade teachers to see their work so excellently adapted by members of the calibre of Corporal Templeton."

Personality of the week

Mr James Parker Templeton of 201 Newtown Road, Carlisle, is a man you might only meet up with during some dire emergency such as an accident or a fire.

But this being the case you would be very pleased to see him, for he is a trained fireman and ambulanceman, holder of the Queen's Long Service Medal for firemen with 29 years service, and of the Queen Victoria Long Service Medal for St. John Ambulance.

He was born at Belle Vue, Carlisle, in the house in which his sister, Mrs Marion Reid, now lives with their 92 year old father.

After attending Newtown and Ashly Street schools, he left and began his apprenticeship with a fabric firm, who used to be where Dixons chimney is today. Mr Templeton qualified as a textile designer and engineer and eventually became a Fellow of the Textile institute.

His interest in first aid and sick nursing began back in September 1937, when he joined the Carlisle division of the St. John Ambulance Brigade - an interest that was later to decide his way of life. He was called up into an infantry regiment when war broke out, but immediately transferred to the Royal Army Medical corps with the rank of corporal as soon as it was known he had done some medical training.

From corporal he was promoted to acting Sergeant and was sent first to Abyssinia, then to Egypt and thence to the heart of the Sudan to work on ant-malaria research. He remained there for 18 months in temperatures up to 120 F. in the shade and showed no signs of malaria himself until after he had returned home.

The war took him right through the Western Desert and he left Tripoli for the landings at salerno, arriving with the 3rd Battalion the Coldstream Guards and the 1st battalion the Scots Guards. Losses were sever, but he says that there are still a few survivors in Carlisle today.

Whilst attending the wounded at the famous Red Beach, Salerno, he was taken prisoner by the 16th Panzer Division, remaining captive for three days until it was discovered that the german captors themselves had been forced to retreat, leaving him and his colleagues free once more.

Back in "civvy" street, he forsook his career in textile designing for a post in the City Ambulance Service and remained with them until they were absorbed into the Fire Service in 1949.

"Possibly I would have remained as a skilled ambulanceman", he says, "except for the fact that my boss pointed out the advantages of being a fireman, with a lower retirement age and better pension. He sent me to fire School at Newcastle. I passed the course and became a fireman."

It is quite unique for one man to hold both the Queens Long Service Medal for firemen and the Queen Victoria Long Service Medal for ambulancemen - especially as the latter carries three bars each representing five years service, and a fourth bar is due to be added shortly.

Married with a family of three daughters - Frances (17), Elizabeth (14) and Ann (4) - Mr Templeton is busy compiling a book about old Carlisle in his spare time and is on the lookout for pictures or photographs of the city prior to the 1928 pageant.

RETIRED

Now retired and living at 201 Newtown Road I began to build up my photographic collection of Carlisle and the Cumberland area (now Cumbria).

Also to collect as much historical information about Carlisle and the County as possible, so at this period I travelled many miles with the late Tom Gray, County Archivist. We were privileged to have permission to walk into many of the key places such as Corby Castle, Netherby Hall, Greystoke, Naworth, Dacre, etc. and read through rare books and take photographs of interest.

Many of the people whose ancestors were nobility and land owners such as Colonel Levin (Lawson) of Corby and the Grahams of Netherby and many others were of great assistance.

The public as a whole were of great assistance also sending photographs and supplying information about the city and county area and events of long ago.

It took a lot of time and patience handling old post cards, photographs and photo plates and bringing these back to life.

My parents were still alive and living in Belle Vue at 38 Moorhouse Road, my father was still painting water colour pictures, so I fancied my chances at painting water colours also; a case of the son trying to outdo the master. However I got started and learned the hard way, father was a hard critic when it came to painting pictures but a true and honest tutor.

James Father & Mother
Mr & Mrs D Templeton outside
6 Belmont Terrace, Belle Vue, Carlisle
at the time of their Golden wedding.

My sister Marion

59

He would always tell you what he thought good or bad. At one period he met L S Lowry here in Carlisle and after a long chat he said to Lowry "you carry on painting your way, but I would not hang these on my walls, you must have a good imagination".

The River Garry, Glen Garry, Scotland.   By J P Templeton

Father painted what he saw to the best of his ability and was still painting at the age of 90. People who knew my father and his work flatter me when they say I am now painting 'almost' as good as my father. As with my photography I find painting a great pleasure but some days are just not long enough.

During my retirement I have enjoyed every minute with my wife Anne and three daughters roaming the countryside, walking, shooting, fishing, hunting and of course meeting people of all walks of life from Royalty to tramps.

Now I am not trying to beat my father, I am trying to beat the clock and most days are too short to catch up with all the interesting things at stake.

James P Templeton's Dad Mr D Templeton with a nice catch of Caldew trout. Circa 1938.

The Templeton family at Brampton Old Church. Circa 1938.

It's always a mystery to me how some people can sit and do nothing.

Anne has helped me over the years to sort and catalogue the collection over the years and many a day could be spent sorting and searching for a particular negative or print. The old saying two heads are better than one comes to mind.

During our work at home we were often side tracked by people ringing up asking all manner of questions regarding Carlisle and the County. Also seeking copies of old photographs for school projects or people doing a history of their family etc.

D Templeton fishing the Eden   Circa 1950.
Dan Templeton fished all his long life from
the age of 8 until he was 90.
He died aged 96.

We also had students who were doing projects on buildings such as the castle, cathedral etc or Carlisle ship canal and railways. I usually try to help and often learn something I did not know in the process – you're never to old to learn!

Several students have come to say 'thank you for the help' and inform me they have got their degree, its nice to know they have managed so well. I wonder if I will ever get a degree? *(I don't think so!)*.

Father D Templeton getting ready to fish the Caldew.

MEMORIES

If you lived when I was a boy in the late 20s and 30s looking back it is hard to believe we have survived as long as we have.

If you were ill granny or mother would have some old cure from the dark ages – goose grease, turpentine, iodine, zambuck etc; and if it was something very bad you were lucky to survive. There was no child proof lids on medicine bottles, if we rode a bicycle we had no helmets. We spent most of our time outside, and spent hours with pals building go-carts out of scraps of wood and an old pram frame with the wheels on. One thing we never thought of was when we finally got going there was no brakes – 'oh dear'.

Days well spent at the river, fishing the Caldew and Photographing.
As an old friend remarked - "It's a hard life enjoying yourself"!

Often especially during school holidays we would leave home in the morning and play all day as long as we were home before dark. Most of the time we played on the adjoining fields, or the main road as there was almost no traffic. No one was able to reach us, unless they came on foot – there were no mobile phones then.

We had the occasional accident but no one was to blame but us. We had fights at school in the yard (not often), he who dares wins. If you had a punch up and got a black eye or a few bruises you soon got over it.

We ate almost anything, cakes, bread and butter (real farm butter) often with home made jam, drank lemonade or water but we were never overweight because we were always on the go.

Frank Parker and James Parker Templeton waiting for geese on the Solway in winter.

We shared a drink with our pals from one bottle and no one died from this because we were healthy!

We had no play stations or televisions, video tapes, DVDs or mobile phones and no computers or adding machines. We had friends and games. We were outside with our friends and always found a game to play.

House doors were always open – you just rang and walked in for a cup of tea or a chat.

We played football a lot sometimes not everyone made the team, those who did not get a game had to learn to live with the disappointment!

If you did do anything wrong you were liable to get a 'clout' round the ear and that was the end of it.

63

Captain Banks K.O.R.B.R and James with the new figure of John Peel and one of his hounds. The figure met with my approval as being correct on the second run.

When the winter snows fell and Bell Vue hill was frozen, we would find a board, an old bath tub or a bogey with no wheels and sledge down the hill from top to bottom towards Burgh Road or the other side towards Acredale.

A Cumberland Lad.

Or we would make a long slide on the hill and set off with our clogs on, these were good on the hard snow or ice – but not so good on the trouser bottoms!

These hard winter days seem a thing of the past, many a time the Lough at Monkhill or Thurstonfield would be frozen for weeks, and those who could skate enjoyed the icy conditions.

Carlisle Great Fair 1976 James and Anne his daughter and some Carlisle firemen wearing old time dress and brass helmets.

64

SOLWAY SPACEMAN

A family day out that has lasted 42 years, all because of a simple photograph.

The date was 23rd May 1964 and the Templeton family decided to go for a day out to the marsh near Burgh-by-Sands. Mam, Dad, Frances and Elizabeth: on arriving there the day was fine and bright but with no sunshine.

We decided to take some photographs especially as Elizabeth was wearing a new dress of bright colours. So while she was gathering sea pinks I began to take several photographs.

We had a pleasant day out on the marsh, nothing out of the ordinary, just a family day out.

I sent my spool of photographs to the local developer and printer and they in turn sent the colour film to Kodak for processing. When it came back I went to collect it from the Photographic Depot on West Walls. The Manager said "we have had a peep at your photographs, they are nice on Kodak's new Gold Film and there is a nice photograph of Elizabeth, but it's rather spoilt by the Big Man' behind her. Who is he?"

Yes, who is he? We are still asking that question 42 years on!

All I can say at this moment of time is that the photograph is <u>not a fake</u>.

(It was on Kodak Gold Colour Film, processed by Kodak and Kodak took full responsibility for the developing and printing).

After the photograph was published in various papers, local, national and international we started to get correspondence from all over the world. Many wanted a copy of the photograph and I duly obliged by posting one to them. It was not easy to recoup the cost of the print and postage in some cases so we asked for sets of stamps of the country they were being sent to, as Frances (our eldest daughter) was a keen stamp collector at the time.

From: Captain George Cordle, Grenadier Guards
Temporary Equerry to H.R.H. The Duke of Edinburgh

BUCKINGHAM PALACE

13th May, 2002.

Dear Mr Templeton,

The Duke of Edinburgh has asked me to thank you for your letter.

His Royal Highness was most interested to see the photograph of your daughter which I am returning herewith for safe-keeping.

Prince Philip sends you his best wishes.

Yours Sincerely
George Cordle

Manchester, Blenheim, Glastonbury, Dunbarton, Middlesex, Cardiff, Brighton, London, Mansfield, Moffat, Penrith, Newport, Edinburgh, Newmarket, Solihull, Sidcup and Yarmouth are just a sample of places in the UK where an interest was shown.

Amazingly we also received correspondence from Cleveland, Ohio in USA; New South Wales, Australia; Stockholm, Sweden; Denmark; Barcelona, Spain; Geneva, Switzerland; California, USA; Quebec, Canada; Ontario, Canada; Pennsylvania, USA; Changi, Singapore; Seville, Spain and Prague, Czechoslovakia to name but a few.

Solway 'spaceman' poses picture puzzle for police experts

By a Staff Reporter

AN amazing photograph from a family outing, which also shows in the background the figure of a man dressed in a white " space suit," has mystified Carlisle City and the County Police.

The photograph was taken on a beautiful clear day on Burgh Marsh by Mr James Templeton, of 201 Newtown Road, a member of the Carlisle Fire Service, who does official photographic work for the service.

Mr Templeton was on a quiet outing with his wife and two daughters when he took what he thought was a perfectly ordinary snapshot of his youngest daughter, Elizabeth, aged five, sitting on the side of a small creek.

A shock

But when the photograph was developed it provided a shock.

The film was sent away to the Kodak Colour Processing Laboratories, and when it was returned to a local firm, it was pointed out to Mr Templeton that one of the best pictures had been " spoiled by the man in the background wearing a space suit "

Mr Templeton told the " Cumberland News " yesterday: " I thought the girl assistant was joking at first, because there was not another soul in the vicinity when I took the photograph — but there was the figure.

The figure is standing about eight yards behind my little girl, and it can be seen fairly clearly on the photograph. It was thought to be a man dressed in a white space suit."

The spot

Describing the spot where he took the photograph, he said: " You look straight across to Chapelcross Atomic Energy Station, and if you turn your head and shoulders to the left you look straight at the V.L.F. Station at Anthorn. The picture I took was not dead in line with Chapelcross."

Mr Templeton approached the Carlisle Division of the Cumberland, Westmorland and Carlisle Constabulary about his amazing photograph and the film and print were forwarded to Police Headquarters at Carleton Hall, Penrith for examination by photographic experts.

30 years

Mr Templeton, who has been a keen amateur photographer for more than 30 years said: " The figure appears to be wearing a white padded suit of some kind, and he is wearing a protective headgear which could be perspex, because you can see the outer glow of it and the dark outline of the side of his head.

" He is standing with one hand on his hip and the body is solid."

It was too good a photograph for the figure to have been caused by any blemish on the film. He had been informed by the film company that it was impossible for any exposure to be made on a new film before being sold.

Mr Templeton was quite adamant that there were no trees or water reflection which could have interfered, nor was there anything on the skyline or any other photographic aspect.

" It just cannot be fathomed. It is just part and parcel of the photograph. The image of the man is definitely part of the negative."

He said that the nearest people to the family on the Marsh where the photograph was taken were an elderly couple sitting in a car reading a newspaper.

" A minute after I took that particular snap I took another photograph of Elizabeth almost on the same spot, and there was nothing unusual on it. The background was perfectly clear."

The picture was taken on Kodacolour X at 100th of a second at f16.

Mr Templeton said he had been back to the Marsh since and had stood on the spot where the figure was shown.

" They say the camera

(Continued on Page 13)

66

Mr and Mrs Templeton and the camera which snapped the "spaceman."
(Report and picture Page One.)

'Spaceman' poses a puzzle

(Continued from Page One)

doesn't lie, but this makes you wonder," Mr Templeton added.

Supt. Donald Roy, of the Carlisle City Police, said he had seen the photograph, and added: "I don't know the answer to this one."

He continued: "One sees a figure there which is definitely human, but there appear to be striations on the film, and if you look further along it you see them again. I would not say that there is any definition of a space suit."

Supt. Roy said one person had put forward the theory that it was a mirage. "If you look across Burgh Marsh on a very clear and hot day you

get the effect of expanse of land, sand and sea, and it might well be something has arisen from that."

Supt. Tom Oldcorn, head the C.I.D. at Carleton Hall Headquarters, to whom the film and print were forwarded by the Carlisle Division, said a file had been opened on the matter.

"My photograph men have had a look at the print and film, and the feeling is that someone else has got into the picture."

But Mr Templeton remains quite adamant that no one but Elizabeth was in front of the camera when he took the fantastic snap.

Police officials at Carleton

Hall last night told Mr Templeton that they had "gone into every possible photographic angle and theory they knew" and could not find a satisfactory answer to the picture.

Mr Templeton said they had asked him whether it was possible that his wife could have stepped into the picture. Mr Templeton said this was not possible: she had been standing behind him holding their other child's hand.

*Press Cuttings
from 1964*

After the publication of the photograph and investigations into its authenticity by the local police labs the photograph was checked out by Kodak and the camera checked out for faults too.

All was as it should be and Kodak were confident it was not a fault with their equipment and said if anyone could find fault with them or their paper, film etc. they would supply them with equipment for life. So they were confident.

Some days after the photograph was printed in Australian newspapers we had correspondence from a technician who had been on the countdown for the Blue Streak missile in Woomera, Southern Australia (also in May 1964). He and his colleague were on leave and had seen the photograph and wanted a copy to show his superiors as they had seen the self same figure on their monitor in the launch area of the missile. Subsequent searches had found no-one there and they were sent on leave to rest!

The suited figure in our photograph was exactly what they had seen in the launch area, but they had seen two figures.

Interest increased and speculation as to what we had 'seen' grew.

I was on duty at the Fire Station one morning in August 1964 when two official looking men wearing black suits and bowler hats walked in. They asked my superior officer if they could speak with me and I was given the ok to go with them to the site where I took the photograph some months earlier on Burgh Marsh. I asked where they were from but was told I did not need to know except that they were from Her Majesty's Government. They showed me to their Jaguar and drove in silence to the marsh.

When we passed the sign for Burgh by Sands one of them got agitated and remarked "are we on the right Road, that sign says 'Burg'".

After passing along the marsh we stopped at the place where the photograph was taken, walked a short way to the exact spot, we stopped and I pointed to the place where Elizabeth had sat. One of them then said "so this is where you saw the large man, an alien".

I replied that we never saw anyone. He said "Oh, you didn't see any man' then he turned and headed back to the car with his colleague they got in and drove off.

In those days I occasionally smoked a pipe so I wandered towards the road expecting they would turn on Easton Bridge but they didn't, they just drove off. That was the last I saw of them. I began to walk back towards Dykesfield and managed to get a lift back to Carlisle.

We heard no more of the 'men in black', why they had visited or who had sent them. (I wasn't sure if I really wanted to know).

We returned to the site a year to the day later and took photographs of the girls but these were never developed. We received the negatives back with the relevant photographs cut out and the remainder cellotaped back together telling us 'not to pursue the matter'.

For some time we sent our photographs away in the name of friends and neighbours so as not to have them ruined.

The anniversary of the photograph was nearly always marked in the press by TV coverage and/or coverage in the tabloids.

Some years later in 1996 a UFO researcher called Jenny Randles made some in depth investigations into the 'Solway Spaceman' and the Woomera incident at the Public Records Office in London. The incident was over the 30 years and papers on the case would be made available to the public but she drew a blank in many quarters. She did however decide that someone somewhere must have been interested in it at some time for the relevant files to be blocked or missing.

It is up to you to draw your own conclusions. I am sure someone out there knows what it was and where it was from.

JIM TEMPLETON'S TEMPLE

What a joy it is to pay a visit to 201 Newtown Road
In this Holy sanctum lair.
There is treasure I do declare,
Photo's, painting, marquatary rare
Standing down with date flair.
Enter by the front door
Sneak a glance towards the left
Wall stands an impressive kilted
Figure caught by camera's eye in moment rare.

Cumberland's claim to canny cap all is refloated on every wall.
Jim sir – and Anne work well together
It needs an angel after all
To see Jim's treasures in 'sec' a clutter;
So some dames would just stand and mutter,
Ad consign t'lot to the grassings grave.

A quick peep through the kitchen window,
Where by Jim's guile is built a chuff aw housing a
Volkswagon supremely unique
Which has covered kilometres by the hundred thousand
Surely by now it is antique.

Carels past might have been veiled in mystery if by chance
Jim had a bower been
The Cumberland News would have had space to spare,
If Jim boys queries had not been printed in there.

Visual exhibitions of Jim's photographic art
Has gladdened the hearts of audiences far apart.
Five hundred shows Anne Templeton informed me
As I bit my tongue to refrain from saying 'get away'
Pray accept my humble effort call it Arther Holmes poetic lay.

Lay Sir Walter Scott's word for his minstrel cantors.

By Arthur Holmes - Age 90

GENERAL

While on a visit to Corby Castle in 1999 with Anne, my wife, we were chatting to Mr and Mrs Haughey (now Lord and Lady Ballyedmond) and after a pleasant conversation Edward smiled and said, "is there anything you have not done?"

I said, "Oh yes, I have never been off the ground." Edward was amazed I had never flown. "I will fix that" he said. He promptly lifted the telephone and made a short call, turned to Anne and I and said, "my pilot is ready to fly you both in the helicopter over Carlisle and the Solway whenever you are ready".

How could we refuse such an offer? So we both went on a short flight over the city and Solway area. It was breath taking to see the city and county from the air! A new experience for us both.

In February 2005, at 85, I flew for the first time on a passenger jet from Prestwich to Murcia in Spain with my daughter Frances and grandson Andrew. Quite an experience but very enjoyable, so much so I had to give it another go just to make sure it was that good! When Frances asked if I would like to go again I was delighted to say yes. So on October 25th we flew from Edinburgh to Alicante this time, the warm climate is certainly an added attraction.

Who knows this flying might catch on!

First experience of flying 1999.

70

J P Templeton signing autographs in the Fire Station Yard, Carlisle 1964.

James signing some of his first books in W.H. Smith.
Photograph by Cumbrian Newspapers Ltd.

Turning over a new leaf

WHEN Carlisle fireman Jim Templeton retired after 25 years' service he decided to turn author.

And yesterday he was autographing copies of his second pictorial record of old Carlisle at W. H. Smith's.

During his years in the fire service, Mr. Templeton of Newtown Road, attended more than 1,500 major road accidents.

Pictured (left) with Mr. Templeton is 16-year-old Christine Norman, of Kirkbride, who assisted him during the signing session.

Jim's exhibition takes positive view

"NICE photograph," said an assistant at a Carlisle photographic store to a customer, referring to a print of a wintry Lakeland scene.

"It would look nice above my fire. Do you have any more?" she asked, not realising she was talking to one of the area's best-known photographers. Jim Templeton.

The manager, who knew him, chipped in: "He's probably got a couple of thousand."

Thanks to sponsorship from that firm and several others locally, everyone can now enjoy a sample of work from the collection.

Reflections of the Past, on show at Carlisle's Tullie House until July 20, contains examples of Jim's own work and that of other cameramen, taken in Cumbria and gathered over his lifetime.

"It is really a dream come true having a sample of the collection on show — and I just

● **ALMOST ALL MY OWN WORK:** Jim Templeton proudly surveys his exhibition. Visitors can buy a set of black-and-white prints
Picture: STEWART BLAIR

hope that people will enjoy coming along and seeing the prints," said Jim, 77.

Jim has carried a camera with him since the age of about 11, and possesses thousands of negatives. His favourite is a shot of sunset on the Solway.

"I went there every night for three weeks before I got it just right," he recalled.

Most interest is still likely to focus on a photograph that Jim took of his daughter Elizabeth on Burgh marshes over 30 years ago — and which has

been seen worldwide.

The photograph features what appears to be a spaceman behind his daughter — a phenomenon still unexplained.

A photography competition is running alongside the exhibition until May 11.

Charlie Emett and James Templeton

HOLIDAYS

Holidays were not the big thing they are nowadays, instead of jetting off to foreign shores we holidayed a bit nearer home, but they were fun and a break from working just the same.

When the girls were younger holidays were Silloth or Allonby, sometimes in a cottage or sometimes in a caravan. I don't know if I am imagining it but the weather seemed to be better then on home shores than it is now!

Sandcastles and walks along the sea front at Silloth, donkey rides and Twentyman's

ice cream at Allonby (some things haven't changed).

As the girls got older we ventured further afield to see old friends in Scotland. The roads were quieter with far fewer cars and people didn't seem to be in such a hurry to get places.

An army friend in Dysart invited us to stay and tour around the Fife coast area. A beautiful part of the world and one we returned to many times. Visits to Pittenweem, Anstruther, St Andrews, Largo and many other coastal areas were very picturesque and visited often. The girls knew once they spied the Forth Road Bridge we were nearly there!

The girls got older and holidayed with friends – times move on and it was some time before Anne and I got back to regular holiday breaks. We nearly always travelled north to Scotland, by car at first but mostly by coach which was more enjoyable for me, being able to take in the scenery. Our favourite tours were with Highland Heritage Tours.

We have been on a lot of their tours and it was difficult to find somewhere we had not been. We found Orkney and some of the other Isles were beautiful and loved to go there – apart from the midges!

One of our favourite tours was to The Highland Hotel at Crianlarich, the bedrooms were along narrow corridors and a large dog had a habit of sleeping across the passage. To get to our room we often had to step over him, Anne first with me holding her hand, hoping he would not decide to get up. We laughed saying she would end up riding him he was so big!

Later correspondence with Ian Cleaver of Highland Heritage we found the dog was an African Ridgeback by the name of 'Muttley' who was not always popular with all the guests!

Sadly when Anne became ill we settled for visits to family in Scotland where our eldest daughter lives, but these were just as enjoyable.

Now of course, as I have mentioned previously, I have joined the 'jet set' and have been to Spain twice and am presently looking forward to my third visit before the winter! If only Scotland had the weather we would not need to fly!

SPECIAL NOTE

Many people have a hobby of some sort – golf, bowling, chess, photography and many more. This keeps the mind active and gives an interest.

I find my retired life is just as busy as when I was working, it is so sad when you hear someone say life is so boring once retired there's only the television. I often wonder how I had time to go to work. The days are not long enough for me, the only worry I have I know I will never finish some of the things I would like to complete.

To the public I am best known for photography and knowledge of old Carlisle and Cumberland but not many people will know me as a water colour artist. This I enjoy very much because it makes you aware of the landscape and ever changing light and sky. I still try to match my father's work and skill as an artist.

James with one of his watercolours.

James P Templeton. Armistice 2005.

*Photograph of Jimmy Shand
by J P Templeton.*

*The Boys, Eric Wallace and James Templeton.
We met many times doing programmes on Border News and Lookaround*

ROYALTY

This Photograph was taken when H.R.H Princess Alexander came to Carlisle to unveil the plaque for the New Lanes, the event in Scotch Street was almost at an end suddenly she turned round and came towards the car and saw me talking to Mr. Arthur the driver. She wanted to know where she could buy a broad camera strap, the same as the one on my camera, I offered her the one I was wearing.
Her reply - It's a kind offer but I will buy one at the shop Wallace-Heatons, London.

This Photograph was taken by the late Bill Walker of The Cumberland News.

James' Carlisle Book specially bound and presented to The Duke of Gloucester on his visit to Carlisle.

H.R.H. The Duchess of York visiting Carlisle.
Photograph by J P Templeton.

BUCKINGHAM PALACE

27th June 1989

Dear Mr Templeton

The Duchess of York has asked me to write and
thank you for your recent letter which she was very
pleased to receive.

Her Royal Highness much appreciated your kind
thought in enclosing the photograph from her visit to
Carlisle. I am to send you Her Royal Highness's
sincere thanks and warmest wishes.

Yours sincerely

Joan G. Lloyd

Lady in Waiting

James and H.R.H. Prince Charles meet at Carlisle Fire Station to discuss previous floods in Carlisle. The floods were mentioned but the main topic was very a different subject. (sorry Confidential). Photograph by Cumbria Constabulary.

I am now 86 years of age and hope to continue photography and painting a little longer, god willing.

One thing I enjoy is talking to people, young or old no matter who they are royalty or rogues, rich or poor, never judge a man by his clothes but by his conversation.

We now live in a troubled world and it would be a better place if all men lived as brothers and paid more attention to nature and the environment.

If I were to live another 86 years I would still do the same things, marry the same lass and have the same family.

I wish you all good health and success in whatever you do.

James Parker Templeton.

CLARENCE HOUSE
LONDON SW1A 1BA

From: The Equerry to HRH The Prince of Wales

14th February, 2005

Dear Mr Templeton,

Thank you for your letter of 9th February to The Prince of Wales. His Royal Highness was very grateful for the history of the Otter Hound and has asked me to thank you for the trouble you have taken to write in.

His Royal Highness was also very grateful for the photograph of your recent meeting in Carlisle.

This letter comes with The Prince of Wales's best wishes.

Yours sincerely,

Squadron Leader Richard Pattle RAF

James Templeton Esq., ATI, FICAP